PARENTING GUIDE MADE SIMPLE

Proven Strategies to Navigate Every Stage of Your Child's Growth

Author: George Martin

ABOUT THE AUTHOR

George Martin, the author of *Parenting Guide Made Simple: Proven Strategies to Navigate Every Stage of Your Child's Growth*, brings an extensive depth of knowledge and practical experience to the realm of parenting. As a professional with years of hands-on expertise in family dynamics, he offers a unique approach to child-rearing that emphasizes the importance of understanding the parent-child relationship from infancy through adolescence.

Martin's professional skills encompass a wide array of parenting methods, grounded in his extensive studies and real-life applications. His insights into effective communication, particularly active listening, are a testament to his understanding of how pivotal it is to foster open dialogue with children. Through his work, he showcases the ability to create a strong foundation of trust and security, an essential component of the parent-child bond that he emphasizes throughout the book.

One of the hallmarks of Martin's expertise is his approach to discipline. He differentiates between discipline and punishment, advocating for positive parenting methods that promote better behavior without resorting to harsh measures. His skills in conflict resolution are particularly valuable, as he offers parents practical tools to manage sibling rivalry and navigate stressful family dynamics with patience and resilience.

Martin's comprehensive knowledge is also evident in his exploration of various child development stages. From nurturing emotional intelligence in toddlers to helping teenagers navigate the complexities of adolescence, his ability to adapt strategies to fit a child's evolving needs stands out. His advice on fostering independence in children, supporting academic growth and preparing teenagers for adulthood shows a clear understanding of how to guide children toward becoming well-rounded individuals.

Moreover, Martin emphasizes the importance of self-care for parents, recognizing that a healthy, balanced approach to parenting not only benefits the child but also the parent. His understanding of the delicate balance between freedom and boundaries during the teenage years highlights his ability to adapt to the ever-changing needs of a child while maintaining necessary limits.

George Martin's book reflects his broad parenting knowledge, rooted in professional training and real-world experiences, offering readers valuable insights into raising confident, compassionate and well-adjusted children.

PREFACE

Parenting is one of life's most rewarding yet challenging journeys. As parents, we constantly strive to nurture, guide and support our children through every stage of their development. Each phase of childhood brings unique joys and hurdles, demanding that we adapt and grow alongside our children. Yet, amidst the overwhelming amount of advice available today, many parents find themselves uncertain about the best path to take.

This book, *Parenting Guide Made Simple: Proven Strategies to Navigate Every Stage of Your Child's Growth*, aims to be a comprehensive, practical and easy-to-follow guide for parents navigating this rewarding journey. Drawing on years of research, insights from child development experts and real-life parenting experiences, this book provides proven strategies to help parents build meaningful relationships with their children, instill essential values and navigate common parenting challenges with confidence.

Organized into five sections, the guide begins by laying the foundations of effective parenting, exploring how to build strong bonds, communicate effectively and discipline positively. It then dives into specific stages of childhood from the playful yet demanding early years to the transformative teenage phase offering age-appropriate strategies for fostering independence, emotional intelligence and resilience. Finally, the book addresses common challenges such as managing sibling rivalry, maintaining balance during stressful times and prioritizing parental self-care.

As a parent myself, I know there is no one-size-fits-all approach to raising children. However, my hope is that the strategies in this book will provide you with tools to tailor your parenting style to your child's unique needs and personality.

George Martin

DEDICATION

I dedicate this book, "Parenting Guide Made Simple: Proven Strategies to Navigate Every Stage of Your Child's Growth," to the extraordinary individuals who have been my unwavering pillars of support and inspiration throughout this journey.

To my beloved parents, who nurtured me with unconditional love, boundless patience and unwavering guidance, thank you for laying the foundation of my values and for teaching me the essence of compassion and resilience. Your belief in me has been the driving force behind all my endeavors and this book is a testament to the lessons you instilled in me.

To my dear family members, whose love and encouragement have always been a source of strength, I am forever grateful for the sense of belonging and unity that you have fostered in our lives. Your unwavering support reminds me daily of the power of family bonds and the importance of nurturing them.

To my incredible friends, who have been my cheerleaders, confidants and guides, thank you for standing by me through thick and thin. Your kindness and wisdom have enriched my life in countless ways, and your encouragement has fueled my passion to create something meaningful for others.

Lastly, to my best wishers, whose belief in my vision has inspired me to push the boundaries of my creativity and knowledge, I extend my heartfelt gratitude. Your trust in my abilities motivates me to share valuable insights with those who seek guidance on this incredible journey called parenting.

This book is a labor of love, a reflection of the countless lessons I have learned from you all and a gift to every parent striving to create a nurturing and empowering environment for their child

Table of Contents

INTRODUCTION

Parenting is often described as one of the most rewarding yet challenging journeys in life. From the moment your child is born, you are tasked with not only ensuring their survival but also guiding them toward becoming healthy, happy and capable individuals. It is a role that evolves as your child grows, requiring continuous learning, adaptation and self-reflection. While every parent dreams of raising confident and compassionate children, the reality is that the path to effective parenting is neither linear nor one-size-fits-all. This is where "Parenting Guide Made Simple: Proven Strategies to Navigate Every Stage of Your Child's Growth" comes in a comprehensive yet approachable resource designed to help you navigate the complexities of raising children with confidence and care.

The Journey of Parenting

Parenting is a journey that begins with uncertainty.

Whether you're a first-time parent or already have children, every stage of your child's growth brings new challenges and questions. From soothing an infant's cries to guiding a teenager through emotional turbulence, each phase is marked by unique milestones, learning experiences and opportunities for growth for both the child and the parent. This book acknowledges the evolving nature of parenting and aims to provide you with practical, proven strategies to help you navigate the ever-changing landscape of your child's development.

At its core, effective parenting is about building a strong, trusting relationship with your child. It is about being present, understanding their needs and providing consistent guidance while allowing them the freedom to explore and grow. However, in today's fast-paced world, where parents juggle multiple responsibilities, maintaining this balance can be overwhelming. The challenges of discipline, communication, emotional support, and even managing your own well-being can often feel daunting. This guide seeks to simplify these complexities, offering actionable advice and insights grounded in research and real-world parenting experiences.

Why This Book Matters

The journey of raising children is deeply personal, but it is also shaped by universal principles of human development. Over decades, research in psychology, child development, and family dynamics has uncovered strategies that can help parents foster stronger bonds, nurture emotional intelligence and guide children toward positive behaviors. This book distills those insights into accessible and relatable advice, tailored for parents navigating the demands of modern life.

The topics covered in this book span the entire spectrum of parenting from the foundational principles that shape your approach to specific techniques for addressing challenges at each stage of your child's growth. Whether you're learning how to handle toddler tantrums, support your middle schooler's academic journey, or navigate the complexities of teenage independence, this book provides the tools you need to parent with intention, empathy and resilience.

The Structure of This Book

"Parenting Guide Made Simple" is divided into five key sections, each addressing a critical aspect of parenting:

Foundations of Effective Parenting: This section lays the groundwork for successful parenting by helping you understand your parenting style, build a strong parent-child bond, and adopt effective communication and discipline techniques. These foundational principles set the stage for navigating the specific challenges of each developmental phase.
Early Childhood (0-5 Years): Early childhood is a time of rapid growth and discovery, where your child begins to develop emotional intelligence, social skills, and a sense of security. This section provides practical advice on nurturing creativity through play, managing tantrums, and establishing routines that provide structure and confidence.
Middle Childhood (6-12 Years): During this stage, children begin to assert their independence, form

friendships and develop their values. Here, you'll learn strategies to encourage responsibility, foster healthy relationships and support their academic journey while instilling a love for learning.

The Teenage Years (13-18 Years): Adolescence is a period of significant change, both for your child and your relationship with them. This section addresses common challenges like managing teen emotions, setting boundaries while respecting their growing independence, and preparing them for adulthood with essential life skills.

Parenting Challenges and Solutions: No parenting journey is without its hurdles. This section tackles common challenges such as sibling rivalry, parenting through stressful times, and maintaining consistency as a parenting team. It also highlights the importance of self-care, emphasizing that a well-supported parent is better equipped to support their child.

The Goal of This Book

The purpose of this guide is not to dictate a single "right way" to parent but to empower you with knowledge and tools to make informed decisions that align with your family's unique values, circumstances and goals. By addressing the practical aspects of parenting alongside the emotional and relational dynamics, this book aims to help you cultivate a parenting approach that feels authentic, effective and sustainable.

Every chapter is designed to be both informative and actionable, offering real-world examples, step-by-step strategies and reflective prompts to deepen your understanding of your child and yourself. Parenting is as much about guiding your child as it is about growing as an individual and this book encourages you to embrace both aspects of the journey.

A Word of Encouragement

As you embark on or continue this parenting journey, remember that perfection is not the goal presence, patience and persistence are. Every parent makes mistakes and every challenge is an opportunity to learn and grow. Your love, effort, and willingness to adapt are what truly make a difference in your child's life.

Parenting is not a solitary endeavor; it is a shared experience that connects you with countless others who are navigating similar joys and struggles. By seeking knowledge, sharing experiences and remaining open to growth, you are taking a powerful step toward becoming the best parent you can be.

Let this book be your companion, guide and source of inspiration as you navigate the beautiful, complex and transformative journey of parenting. Together, we'll explore strategies to nurture your child's potential, strengthen your family bonds and equip you with the confidence to face the challenges ahead.

Welcome to "Parenting Guide Made Simple: Proven Strategies to Navigate Every Stage of Your Child's Growth" your roadmap to raising happy, healthy and resilient children. Let's begin.

PICTORIAL REPRESENTATIONS OF GOOD PARENTING

Good parenting

Good parenting

Section 1: Foundations of Effective Parenting

CHAPTER ONE

UNDERSTANDING YOUR PARENTING STYLE: HOW IT SHAPES YOUR CHILD'S GROWTH

Parenting is one of the most rewarding yet challenging roles an individual can take on. It involves more than just ensuring your child's basic needs are met; it also requires nurturing their emotional, social and intellectual development. While every parent's approach to raising a child is unique, certain parenting styles have been widely studied and categorized by psychologists. These parenting style authoritative, authoritarian, permissive and neglectful have a significant influence on a child's growth and development, shaping their personality, behavior and overall outlook on life. Understanding your parenting style and its impact can help you create a nurturing environment that fosters your child's potential.

Parenting Styles and Their Characteristics

1. Authoritative Parenting

Authoritative parenting is often considered the most balanced and effective style. Parents in this category are warm, supportive, and responsive while also maintaining clear expectations and boundaries. They encourage open communication, value their child's opinions and offer guidance rather than control. For example, when a child makes a mistake, an authoritative parent will explain why the behavior is inappropriate and suggest better choices for the future.

Children raised by authoritative parents tend to grow up confident, self-disciplined, and socially adept. They are more likely to excel academically, form healthy relationships, and exhibit emotional resilience because they have learned to balance independence with respect for rules.

2. Authoritarian Parenting

Authoritarian parents emphasize strict rules, obedience, and discipline. This style often involves high expectations with little room for flexibility or input from the child. Parents may use punishment as a primary tool for enforcing rules and might show limited warmth or responsiveness. For instance, when a child questions a rule, an authoritarian parent may respond with, "Because I said so," without further explanation.

Children of authoritarian parents may become highly disciplined and obedient but often struggle with low self-esteem, anxiety, or difficulty making decisions independently. They may fear failure or develop a rebellious streak as a response to the rigid environment.

3. Permissive Parenting

Permissive parents are indulgent and lenient, often acting more like friends than authority figures. They provide warmth and affection but set minimal boundaries, allowing children significant freedom. For instance, if a child refuses to do their homework, a permissive parent might ignore the behavior or give in to the child's demands to avoid conflict.

While children of permissive parents often feel loved and supported, they may struggle with self-discipline and accountability. They might exhibit poor academic performance, have difficulty following rules, and experience challenges in managing frustration or disappointment.

4. Neglectful Parenting

Neglectful parenting, also known as uninvolved parenting, is characterized by a lack of responsiveness and involvement. Neglectful parents may provide for their child's physical needs but offer little emotional support, guidance, or supervision. This can stem from various factors, including personal struggles, lack of knowledge about parenting, or limited interest in child-rearing responsibilities.

Children raised by neglectful parents often face

significant challenges, including low self-esteem, poor social skills and academic struggles. They may also develop feelings of abandonment, leading to difficulties in forming healthy attachments and relationships later in life.

How Parenting Styles Shape a Child's Growth

The way you parent profoundly influences your child's emotional, social and cognitive development. Each parenting style creates a distinct environment that affects how a child perceives themselves and interacts with the world.

1. Emotional Development

Parenting styles play a crucial role in shaping a child's emotional well-being. Authoritative parents, who offer both warmth and structure, create a secure environment where children feel valued and understood. This emotional foundation fosters self-confidence, emotional regulation and resilience.

In contrast, children raised in authoritarian

households may internalize feelings of inadequacy or fear, while those with permissive parents might struggle with emotional self-control. Neglectful parenting, on the other hand, can lead to feelings of rejection and an inability to form trusting relationships.

2. Social Skills

Parenting styles also impact a child's ability to navigate social relationships. Authoritative parenting, with its emphasis on communication and mutual respect, equips children with the tools to build strong interpersonal connections. These children are more likely to display empathy, cooperation and conflict resolution skills.

In authoritarian settings, children might struggle with assertiveness, either becoming overly submissive or excessively aggressive. Permissive parenting can result in difficulties respecting boundaries, while neglectful parenting may hinder a child's ability to engage positively with peers.

3. Cognitive Growth

The cognitive development of a child is significantly influenced by the level of stimulation, encouragement, and guidance they receive. Authoritative parents strike a balance between challenge and support, encouraging their child to explore, learn and problem-solve independently. This approach nurtures curiosity and a growth mindset, leading to better academic performance and critical thinking skills.

On the contrary, authoritarian parents may stifle creativity by focusing solely on obedience, while permissive parents might fail to instill the discipline needed for sustained learning. Neglectful parenting often results in a lack of intellectual stimulation, hindering cognitive development.

Finding the Right Balance

No parent fits neatly into a single category; most fluctuate between styles based on circumstances and their child's needs. However, striving for an authoritative approach often yields the most positive outcomes. This involves:

- Setting Clear Expectations: Establish consistent rules and boundaries while explaining their rationale to your child.
- Encouraging Open Communication: Create an environment where your child feels comfortable expressing their thoughts and feelings.
- Providing Emotional Support: Offer love, empathy and understanding, even when addressing misbehavior.
- Promoting Independence: Allow your child to make age-appropriate decisions and learn from their experiences.

Adapting to Your Child's Unique Needs

Each child is different, and what works for one may not work for another. Factors such as temperament, developmental stage and cultural background can influence how your parenting style affects your child. Being attuned to your child's individuality and adjusting your approach accordingly is crucial.

For example, a child with a sensitive temperament may thrive with more reassurance and patience, while a highly independent child might benefit from additional opportunities for autonomy. The key is to remain flexible and responsive, fostering a relationship built on trust and mutual respect.

The Long-Term Impact of Parenting Styles

The effects of your parenting style extend well beyond childhood. They shape your child's self-concept, coping mechanisms, and approach to relationships throughout their life. By fostering a supportive and structured environment, you set the foundation for your child to become a confident, compassionate and capable individual.

Parenting is an ongoing journey of learning and adaptation. Understanding your style and its influence empowers you to make intentional choices that promote your child's growth and well-being. While no parent is perfect, striving for balance and prioritizing your child's needs ensures that you guide them toward a fulfilling and successful future.

CHAPTER TWO

BUILDING A STRONG PARENT-CHILD BOND: THE FOUNDATION OF TRUST AND SECURITY

The parent-child bond is one of the most vital relationships in human life. It not only shapes the emotional and psychological well-being of the child but also lays the groundwork for their relationships and interactions in adulthood. A strong parent-child bond is built on trust, communication, love and it creates a sense of security that is crucial for the child's growth and development. In today's fast-paced world, fostering this bond requires intentionality, patience and a deep understanding of its importance.

Understanding the Importance of the Parent-Child Bond

The bond between a parent and child serves as the foundation for emotional stability and resilience. This relationship provides children with their first experiences of love, care, and acceptance. When nurtured properly, it helps children feel valued and understood, instilling a sense of self-worth and confidence.

From infancy, children rely on their parents for basic needs like food, warmth and comfort. However, as they grow, their emotional and psychological needs become equally significant. Children who have a secure attachment with their parents are more likely to develop healthy coping mechanisms, form positive relationships, and exhibit better academic and social outcomes. Conversely, a weak or strained bond can lead to feelings of insecurity, anxiety and behavioral issues.

The Role of Trust in Strengthening the Bond

Trust is the cornerstone of any strong relationship, and the parent-child bond is no exception. Building trust begins early in a child's life. Responding consistently to an infant's cries, providing comfort and meeting their needs promptly instill a sense of safety. Over time, this trust deepens as parents show reliability and transparency in their interactions with their children.

For older children, trust is cultivated through open communication and mutual respect. Parents who listen attentively to their children's concerns, validate their feelings and maintain promises demonstrate that they are dependable and understanding. Trust also requires honesty acknowledging mistakes, apologizing when necessary and creating an environment where children feel safe expressing their thoughts without fear of judgment or punishment.

Fostering Emotional Security

Emotional security is vital for a child's mental health and development. A secure child feels loved, protected, and valued, which enables them to explore the world confidently. Parents can foster emotional security by providing consistent care, setting clear boundaries, and offering unconditional love.

Consistency is particularly important. Children thrive when they know what to expect from their parents.

Predictable routines, fair discipline, and a stable home environment create a sense of order and reliability. This stability reassures children that they are safe, even in challenging circumstances.

Additionally, setting clear and age-appropriate boundaries helps children understand acceptable behavior and consequences. Boundaries, when enforced with love and patience, teach children self-discipline and respect for others while maintaining their sense of security.

Unconditional love is perhaps the most powerful tool for fostering emotional security. Regardless of their behavior or achievements, children need to feel that their parents love and accept them. Expressing affection through words, actions, and quality time reinforces this message and strengthens the bond.

The Role of Communication in Strengthening Bonds

Effective communication is the backbone of a healthy parent-child relationship. Open and honest communication fosters understanding, empathy, and trust. It allows parents to connect with their children on a deeper level and provides a safe space for children to express themselves.

Active listening is a key aspect of effective communication. Parents should strive to listen without interrupting, judging or dismissing their child's feelings. Reflecting back what the child says and showing empathy helps them feel heard and understood.

It is also essential to adapt communication styles based on the child's age and developmental stage. For young children, using simple language and visual aids can help them understand concepts. For teenagers, fostering discussions that encourage critical thinking and respecting their opinions promotes mutual respect and trust.

Non-verbal communication, such as body language, facial expressions, and tone of voice, also plays a significant role. A warm smile, gentle touch, or reassuring tone can convey love and support even without words.

Spending Quality Time Together

In the hustle and bustle of daily life, finding time to connect with children can be challenging. However, spending quality time together is crucial for building a strong bond. Shared activities create opportunities for meaningful interactions and strengthen the emotional connection between parents and children.

Quality time does not always require elaborate plans or expensive outings. Simple activities like reading a book, playing a game, cooking a meal, or taking a walk can be deeply enriching. What matters most is the parent's undivided attention and genuine engagement during these moments.

Additionally, celebrating milestones, creating family traditions and participating in shared hobbies help create lasting memories and deepen the bond. These experiences also teach children the value of relationships and the importance of prioritizing loved ones.

Overcoming Challenges in Building a Strong Bond

Building and maintaining a strong parent-child bond is not without its challenges. Modern life often presents obstacles such as busy schedules, technology distractions and differing parenting styles. However, these challenges can be addressed with conscious effort and adaptability.

For instance, parents can establish designated family times, such as shared meals or screen-free evenings, to foster connection. Balancing work and family responsibilities may require prioritizing tasks, delegating duties, or seeking external support.

Conflicts are inevitable in any relationship, but how they are handled can significantly impact the bond. Addressing disagreements with calmness, empathy, and a focus on resolution teaches children valuable conflict-management skills and reinforces trust.

The Lifelong Impact of a Strong Parent-Child Bond

The benefits of a strong parent-child bond extend far beyond childhood. Children who grow up feeling loved and supported are more likely to become resilient, compassionate, and emotionally intelligent adults. They tend to have healthier relationships, better mental health and a greater capacity for empathy and understanding.

Moreover, a strong bond creates a lasting connection between parents and children, even as they grow older. It ensures that children feel comfortable seeking guidance and support from their parents throughout their lives, fostering a relationship based on mutual respect and love.

Conclusion

Building a strong parent-child bond is a continuous journey that requires time, effort, and commitment. It involves nurturing trust, fostering emotional security, maintaining open communication and spending quality time together. While challenges may arise, the rewards of a loving and secure parent-child relationship are immeasurable.

By investing in this bond, parents not only provide

their children with a strong foundation for growth and success but also create a legacy of love and connection that lasts a lifetime. Ultimately, a strong parent-child bond is not just about raising well-adjusted childrenit is about building a relationship rooted in trust, understanding and unconditional love.

CHAPTER THREE

THE ART OF ACTIVE LISTENING: COMMUNICATING EFFECTIVELY WITH YOUR CHILD

Effective communication is at the heart of every healthy parent-child relationship and active listening is one of the most powerful tools a parent can wield in fostering trust, connection and understanding. Children, like adults, crave to be heard and understood, and when parents truly listen, it not only strengthens their bond but also empowers the child to express themselves openly and confidently. However, active listening is more than just hearing words; it's a skill that requires patience, empathy and mindfulness.

This article explores the art of active listening, its benefits, and practical ways to integrate it into everyday interactions with your child.

What is Active Listening?

Active listening is a conscious effort to not only hear the words your child is saying but to understand their emotions, intentions and underlying messages. It involves fully focusing on the speaker, withholding judgment, and responding thoughtfully. Unlike passive listening, where a parent may simply nod or give superficial responses, active listening requires deep engagement and genuine attention.

Active listening involves the following key components:

1. Paying Attention: Giving undivided attention, free of distractions.
2. Body Language: Maintaining open and encouraging non-verbal cues, such as eye contact, nodding, or leaning slightly forward.
3. Clarification and Reflection: Asking questions to ensure understanding and summarizing what the child has expressed.
4. Empathy: Showing understanding and validating their feelings, even if you don't agree with their perspective.

Why is Active Listening Important?

Active listening offers numerous benefits for both parents and children. These include:

1. Building Trust and Connection

When children feel heard, they develop a sense of trust in their parents. This trust creates a safe space where they feel comfortable sharing their thoughts, fears, and dreams. A child who knows they are genuinely listened to is more likely to turn to their parents during times of need.

2. Encouraging Emotional Development

By actively listening to your child, you validate their emotions and teach them how to identify and articulate their feelings. This helps them develop emotional intelligence, a critical skill for building healthy relationships and navigating life's challenges.

3. Resolving Conflicts

Active listening can be a powerful tool for de-escalating conflicts. Instead of reacting emotionally, parents who listen calmly can better understand the root of the issue and work with their child to find a resolution.

4. Boosting Confidence

When parents listen attentively, children feel valued and understood. This boosts their self-esteem and encourages them to express themselves confidently, knowing their voice matters.

5. Modeling Effective Communication

Children learn communication skills by observing their parents. By demonstrating active listening, you teach your child how to listen empathetically to others, fostering respect and understanding in their relationships.

Barriers to Active Listening

Despite its importance, many parents struggle with active listening due to common challenges such as:

1. Distractions: Work, household chores or electronic devices can pull your attention away from the conversation.
2. Judgment: Jumping to conclusions or making assumptions about what your child is saying can hinder understanding.
3. Interruptions: Speaking over your child or finishing their sentences sends a message that

their words are not important.

4. Time Constraints: Busy schedules can make it difficult to dedicate time for meaningful conversations.

Recognizing these barriers is the first step toward improving your listening skills and creating a more open and supportive communication environment.

Practical Tips for Active Listening

Here are actionable strategies to help you become an effective active listener with your child:

1. Create a Distraction-Free Zone

When your child approaches you to talk, set aside distractions like your phone or television. Sit down at their eye level and focus entirely on them. This simple gesture shows that their words are your priority.

2. Use Open-Ended Questions

Encourage your child to express themselves by asking open-ended questions such as:

- "How did that make you feel?"

- "What do you think about that?" This approach invites them to share more, rather than giving one-word answers.

3. Validate Their Feelings

Even if you don't agree with your child's viewpoint, acknowledge their emotions. For example, say, "I can see that you're upset about this," or "It sounds like you were really excited about that." This reinforces their feelings as valid and helps them feel understood.

4. Paraphrase and Reflect

Summarize what your child has said to confirm your understanding. For instance, "So you're feeling nervous about the upcoming test because you want to do well, right?" This not only ensures clarity but also shows that you are fully engaged in the conversation.

5. Practice Patience

Let your child express themselves at their own pace without interrupting. Resist the urge to jump in with advice or solutions immediately. Sometimes, they simply need someone to listen.

6. Avoid Judgment or Criticism

Refrain from criticizing or dismissing their concerns, even if they seem trivial to you. Statements like "That's not a big deal" can make them feel unheard and discourage future communication.

7. Follow Up

Show continued interest in your child's life by revisiting conversations. For example, if they shared concerns about a school project, ask later how it turned out. This reinforces your investment in their well-being.

When to Seek Help

While active listening can significantly enhance your relationship with your child, there may be times when they need additional support. If your child consistently struggles to open up or exhibits signs of stress, anxiety, or depression, consider seeking guidance from a counselor or therapist. Active listening is not a substitute for professional help, but it can complement therapeutic efforts by creating a supportive environment at home.

The Long-Term Impact of Active Listening

The effects of active listening extend beyond childhood. Children who grow up feeling heard and understood are more likely to develop strong communication skills, emotional resilience and self-confidence. They also tend to form healthier relationships in adulthood, as they have learned the importance of empathy and effective dialogue.

For parents, practicing active listening fosters a deeper understanding of their child's personality, needs, and aspirations. It transforms everyday interactions into meaningful moments that strengthen the parent-child bond.

The art of active listening is a cornerstone of effective communication with your child. It requires intention, effort, and practice but pays dividends in building trust, fostering emotional development, and creating a harmonious relationship. By making a conscious effort to listen actively, you give your child the invaluable gift of feeling valued, understood, and loved. Over time, this skill not only enhances your parenting but also equips your child with the tools they need to navigate the world with confidence and empathy.

CHAPTER FOUR

DISCIPLINE VS. PUNISHMENT: POSITIVE PARENTING APPROACHES FOR BETTER BEHAVIOR

Parenting is one of the most rewarding yet challenging roles in life. Shaping children into responsible, empathetic and confident individuals requires a blend of patience, guidance and understanding. A critical aspect of parenting is managing behavior and this often sparks the debate of discipline versus punishment. While the terms are sometimes used interchangeably, they represent fundamentally different approaches to addressing undesirable behavior. Positive parenting focuses on discipline over punishment, fostering a healthy parent-child relationship and promoting better long-term behavior.

Understanding the Differences

Discipline is rooted in teaching and guiding children to understand the consequences of their actions. It focuses on helping them learn self-control, responsibility and problem-solving skills. Discipline emphasizes growth and development, encouraging children to internalize values and make better choices independently.

In contrast, punishment is often about imposing penalties for misbehavior. It focuses on control and compliance, typically relying on fear or negative reinforcement to deter unwanted actions. Punishment may address the immediate issue but often fails to teach children why their behavior was inappropriate or how to make better choices in the future.

The fundamental difference lies in the intent: discipline aims to educate, while punishment seeks to reprimand. Positive parenting leans heavily toward discipline, as it is more effective in cultivating lasting behavioral changes and nurturing a child's emotional well-being.

The Drawbacks of Punishment

Punishment, especially when severe or administered

without explanation, can have several negative effects on children.

1. Fear and Resentment
   Punishment often instills fear rather than respect. Children may comply in the short term to avoid further penalties but may develop resentment toward their parents. Over time, this can damage the parent-child relationship and erode trust.
2. Focus on Avoiding Consequences
   Punishment teaches children to avoid getting caught rather than understanding why their behavior was wrong. This can lead to secretive or dishonest behavior as they seek to escape penalties.
3. Emotional Impact
   Harsh punishment, such as yelling or physical discipline, can cause anxiety, low self-esteem, and feelings of unworthiness. Children may internalize the belief that they are inherently "bad," which can affect their emotional development.
4. Lack of Problem-Solving Skills
   Punishment rarely addresses the root cause of misbehavior. Without guidance on how to handle similar situations differently, children may repeat the same mistakes.

The Benefits of Discipline

Discipline, when implemented as part of a positive parenting strategy, focuses on teaching children to understand and regulate their behavior. This approach has several advantages:

1. Teaches Accountability
    Discipline helps children recognize the connection between their actions and consequences. They learn to take responsibility for their behavior and make amends when necessary.
2. Encourages Problem-Solving
    By discussing the reasons behind rules and expectations, discipline encourages critical thinking and problem-solving. Children learn how to make better choices in the future.
3. Builds Emotional Intelligence
    Discipline fosters empathy and emotional awareness. Children understand how their actions affect others and develop the ability to manage their emotions effectively.
4. Strengthens Parent-Child Relationships
    A discipline-based approach emphasizes communication, respect, and understanding. This strengthens the bond between parent and child, creating a safe environment for learning and growth.

Key Principles of Positive Discipline

Positive discipline relies on consistency, empathy and proactive strategies. Here are some essential principles:

1. Set Clear Expectations
   Children need to understand the boundaries and rules of acceptable behavior. Communicate these expectations clearly and consistently, ensuring they are age-appropriate and realistic.
2. Use Natural and Logical Consequences
   Rather than arbitrary punishments, allow children to experience the natural or logical consequences of their actions. For example, if they refuse to wear a coat, they may feel cold outside. These experiences teach valuable lessons without the need for reprimand.
3. Model the Behavior You Want to See
   Children learn by observing their parents. Demonstrate kindness, patience, and respect in your interactions. By modeling positive behavior, you set a powerful example for your child to follow.
4. Focus on Positive Reinforcement
   Reward and praise good behavior to encourage its repetition. Positive reinforcement helps children feel valued and motivates them to meet expectations.

5. Maintain Open Communication
   Encourage your child to express their thoughts and feelings. Listen actively and validate their emotions, even when addressing misbehavior. Open communication fosters mutual respect and trust.
6. Be Consistent
   Consistency is critical in discipline. Mixed messages can confuse children and undermine the effectiveness of your approach. Stick to established rules and consequences to provide a sense of stability.

Practical Strategies for Positive Discipline

Implementing positive discipline requires thoughtful strategies tailored to your child's age and temperament. Here are some practical tips:

1. Redirection for Young Children
   For toddlers and preschoolers, redirect their attention to a different activity when they exhibit undesirable behavior. This helps them shift focus and prevents escalation.
2. Time-In Instead of Time-Out
   Rather than isolating your child during a time-out, try a time-in approach. Sit with them and discuss their feelings and actions calmly. This reinforces the idea that you are there to

support and guide them.

3. Problem-Solving Together
   Involve your child in finding solutions to behavioral challenges. For instance, if they struggle with sharing, brainstorm ways to take turns with toys. Collaborative problem-solving empowers them to take ownership of their actions.

4. Establish Routines
   Consistent routines help children understand expectations and reduce opportunities for misbehavior. Clear schedules for meals, bedtime, and chores provide structure and predictability.

5. Stay Calm and Patient
   When addressing misbehavior, remain calm and composed. Reacting with anger or frustration can escalate the situation and undermine your message. Take a moment to gather your thoughts before responding.

The Long-Term Impact

Positive discipline is a long-term investment in your child's development. By prioritizing teaching over punishment, you help them grow into empathetic, responsible, and self-aware individuals. They develop a strong moral compass, better interpersonal skills, and the confidence to navigate life's challenges.

Moreover, the positive parenting approach strengthens family relationships. Children raised with discipline rather than punishment are more likely to maintain open and trusting relationships with their parents as they grow older. This foundation of mutual respect and understanding lays the groundwork for lifelong connections.

Discipline and punishment may seem similar, but their effects on children are profoundly different. Positive parenting emphasizes discipline as a means of teaching and guiding children toward better behavior. By focusing on empathy, communication, and consistency, parents can nurture their child's emotional well-being and foster long-term growth. While punishment may yield immediate compliance, it often comes at the cost of emotional health and the parent-child bond. Discipline, on the other hand, builds a solid foundation for responsible and respectful behavior, making it the cornerstone of positive parenting.

CHAPTER FIVE

NURTURING EMOTIONAL INTELLIGENCE IN TODDLERS: THE KEY TO EARLY SOCIAL SKILLS

Emotional intelligence (EI) is a vital component of a child's development, especially in the formative toddler years when foundational social and emotional skills begin to emerge. Emotional intelligence refers to the ability to recognize, understand, and manage emotions in oneself and others. For toddlers, this encompasses recognizing their feelings, regulating their responses and interacting appropriately with their peers and caregivers. By nurturing emotional intelligence during this critical period, parents and caregivers can equip toddlers with essential tools for building strong relationships, navigating social environments, and developing a healthy sense of self.

Understanding Emotional Intelligence in Toddlers

Toddlers experience emotions intensely but lack the vocabulary and understanding to express or regulate them. Emotional intelligence in toddlers often manifests through behaviors, such as sharing toys, responding to a friend's distress or throwing tantrums when frustrated. These behaviors are clues to their budding emotional awareness.

At this age, the brain is rapidly developing, particularly in areas that govern emotional regulation and social interaction. Toddlers are beginning to form neural connections that influence how they perceive and react to emotions. This makes early childhood an ideal time to nurture emotional intelligence, as these early experiences will have long-term implications on their social skills and emotional well-being.

The Role of Emotional Intelligence in Social Skills

Social skills are intricately tied to emotional intelligence. A toddler's ability to connect with others depends on their capacity to understand and respond to social cues, empathize with others, and communicate effectively. Emotional intelligence provides the foundation for these abilities.

For example, a toddler who can identify when a friend is upset is more likely to offer comfort, strengthening their bond. Similarly, a child who learns to manage their frustration during a game is better equipped to collaborate and resolve conflicts. These are the building blocks of positive social interactions that will serve them throughout their lives.

Strategies for Nurturing Emotional Intelligence in Toddlers

1. Model Emotional Awareness
   Parents and caregivers are toddlers' first teachers. Modeling emotional awareness by openly discussing your emotions and reactions can help toddlers understand their own feelings. For instance, saying, "I feel happy when we play together" or "I'm a little upset because the room is messy, but we can fix it" demonstrates how emotions can be recognized and managed constructively.
2. Teach Emotional Vocabulary
   Toddlers need the words to describe their

emotions. Teaching them phrases like "I'm sad," "I'm angry," or "I'm excited" empowers them to articulate their feelings rather than act them out. Books and storytelling are excellent tools for introducing emotional vocabulary in a relatable and engaging manner.

3. Validate Their Emotions
   Validation helps toddlers feel understood and supported. Instead of dismissing their feelings, acknowledge them. For instance, if a child is upset because they can't have a toy, say, "I understand that you're feeling disappointed because you really wanted the toy." This approach helps them feel heard and teaches them that it's okay to experience emotions.

4. Encourage Empathy
   Empathy is a cornerstone of emotional intelligence. Simple activities like role-playing with dolls or discussing how characters in a story might feel can nurture empathy. Encourage toddlers to notice how others feel by asking questions like, "How do you think your friend feels when you share your toys?"

5. Practice Emotion Regulation
   Toddlers often struggle with managing strong emotions, leading to meltdowns or impulsive behavior. Teach them techniques to calm down, such as deep breathing, counting to five, or taking a moment in a quiet space. Over time, these strategies can help toddlers develop self-regulation skills.

6. Foster Social Interaction
    Opportunities to interact with peers are invaluable for developing social skills. Playdates, group activities, and daycare environments allow toddlers to practice sharing, taking turns, and resolving conflicts. Guided interactions, where adults intervene gently when needed, can help toddlers learn how to navigate social situations.
7. Celebrate Efforts and Progress
    Praise toddlers for showing emotional awareness and social skills. For example, acknowledge their effort when they comfort a friend or use their words instead of crying. Positive reinforcement encourages them to repeat these behaviors.

The Role of Play in Emotional Intelligence

Play is a powerful medium for teaching emotional intelligence. Through imaginative play, toddlers explore emotions and practice social scenarios in a safe and creative environment. For example, pretending to cook a meal together or playing "doctor" allows them to experience cooperation, empathy, and problem-solving.

Additionally, games that involve taking turns, like building blocks or simple board games, teach patience and impulse control key components of emotional regulation.

Challenges in Nurturing Emotional Intelligence

While nurturing emotional intelligence is rewarding, it can also be challenging. Toddlers' limited verbal skills and impulsive nature can make it difficult for them to express or control their emotions. Moreover, each child develops at their own pace, so some may take longer to grasp emotional concepts.

Parents and caregivers may also face their own challenges, such as managing their emotions during stressful moments or finding the time to consistently practice these strategies. Patience and persistence are essential in overcoming these obstacles.

Long-Term Benefits of Emotional Intelligence

The benefits of nurturing emotional intelligence in toddlers extend far beyond childhood. Emotionally intelligent children tend to perform better academically, form healthier relationships, and exhibit greater resilience in the face of challenges. They are better equipped to handle peer pressure, resolve conflicts, and empathize with others, which are crucial skills in both personal and professional spheres. Furthermore, emotional intelligence contributes to mental health. Children who learn to process and regulate their emotions are less likely to experience anxiety, depression or behavioral issues as they grow.

Nurturing emotional intelligence in toddlers is an investment in their future. By teaching them to recognize, understand, and manage emotions, parents and caregivers provide them with tools to navigate the complexities of social interactions and relationships. While the process requires patience and consistent effort, the rewards are immeasurable. Toddlers who develop emotional intelligence not only gain early social skills but also build a foundation for a lifetime of emotional well-being, resilience and meaningful connections.

In an increasingly interconnected world, the ability to understand and connect with others is more valuable than ever. By prioritizing emotional intelligence during the early years, we empower toddlers to grow into compassionate, confident and socially adept individuals who can thrive in any environment.

CHAPTER SIX

HANDLING TANTRUMS GRACEFULLY: A PARENT'S GUIDE TO PATIENCE AND CALM

Parenting is one of the most rewarding journeys in life, but it comes with its challenges. Among the most frustrating and emotional moments are tantrums. These outbursts, often characterized by screaming, crying, stomping and sometimes even physical aggression, can test a parent's patience and resolve. However, tantrums are a natural part of a child's development and an opportunity for growth for both the parent and the child. Mastering the art of handling tantrums gracefully can create a calmer, more connected relationship with your child while equipping them with essential emotional skills. Here's how to navigate these challenging moments with patience and calm.

Understanding the Root Causes of Tantrums

To handle tantrums effectively, it's crucial to understand why they occur. Tantrums are typically a child's way of expressing frustration, unmet needs or overwhelming emotions. Some common triggers include:

1. Emotional Overload: Young children, especially toddlers, are still developing emotional regulation skills. When they experience intense emotions such as anger, sadness or excitement, they might not know how to express them appropriately.
2. Unmet Needs: Hunger, fatigue or discomfort can lower a child's tolerance for frustration, making a tantrum more likely.
3. Communication Barriers: Limited language skills can make it difficult for children to articulate their needs, leading to frustration and emotional outbursts.
4. Desire for Autonomy: As children grow, they strive for independence. When they feel their autonomy is restricted, they may react with a tantrum.
5. Seeking Attention: Sometimes, children use tantrums as a way to gain their caregiver's attention, especially if they feel ignored or overlooked.

Understanding these root causes helps parents respond with empathy rather than frustration.

Preparing for Tantrums: Prevention Is Key

While it's impossible to eliminate tantrums completely, proactive strategies can reduce their frequency and intensity.

1. Set Clear Expectations: Consistent routines and boundaries help children feel secure. When they know what to expect, they are less likely to feel frustrated.
2. Provide Choices: Allowing your child to make small decisions, such as choosing between two snacks or picking a shirt, fosters their sense of independence and reduces power struggles.
3. Address Basic Needs: Ensure your child is well-rested, fed, and comfortable to minimize tantrum triggers related to physical discomfort.
4. Teach Emotional Vocabulary: Help your child name their emotions by using phrases like, "It looks like you're feeling upset because you can't have the toy." Developing emotional awareness empowers them to express their feelings more constructively.
5. Plan Transitions Thoughtfully: Sudden changes in activity can be overwhelming for young

children. Prepare them by giving warnings, such as, "We'll leave the park in five minutes."

Staying Calm During a Tantrum

When a tantrum begins, it's natural to feel overwhelmed or frustrated. However, staying calm is essential for de-escalating the situation and modeling appropriate behavior.

1. Pause and Breathe: Take a deep breath before reacting. This helps you regulate your own emotions and approach the situation with clarity.
2. Avoid Overreacting: Yelling or punishing your child during a tantrum often escalates the behavior. Instead, maintain a neutral tone and demeanor.
3. Validate Their Feelings: Acknowledge your child's emotions without necessarily giving in to their demands. For example, say, "I see that you're very upset right now. It's okay to feel angry."
4. Be Present: Sit with your child or stay nearby, even if they are inconsolable. Your calm presence reassures them that they are safe and loved.
5. Avoid Bribes or Rewards: While it might be tempting to offer a treat to stop the tantrum,

this reinforces the idea that tantrums are a way to get what they want.

Responding Effectively to Different Tantrums

Not all tantrums are the same, and your response may vary depending on the situation.

1. For Attention-Seeking Tantrums: If your child is using a tantrum to gain attention, calmly acknowledge their feelings but avoid excessive engagement. Once the tantrum subsides, provide positive attention for appropriate behavior.
2. For Overstimulation Tantrums: In cases of emotional overload, help your child calm down by removing them from the environment or offering a comforting activity like a hug or quiet time with a favorite toy.
3. For Power Struggles: If the tantrum stems from a desire for control, offer limited choices or compromises. For instance, say, "Would you like to clean up your toys now or in five minutes?"
4. For Frustration Tantrums: Encourage problem-solving by guiding your child through the situation. Say, "Let's figure out how we can fix this together."

Helping Your Child Learn from Tantrums

After a tantrum ends, it's an excellent opportunity to teach your child important lessons about emotions and behavior.

1. Reflect Together: Once your child is calm, discuss what happened. Use simple language like, "You were upset because we had to leave the playground. Next time, we can talk about it instead of yelling."
2. Reinforce Positive Behavior: Praise your child when they handle a situation without a tantrum. For example, say, "I'm so proud of how you asked for help instead of getting upset."
3. Teach Coping Skills: Introduce calming strategies, such as taking deep breaths, counting to ten or squeezing a stress ball.
4. Be a Role Model: Demonstrate healthy ways of managing frustration, such as talking through your feelings or taking a break to cool down.

The Role of Self-Care for Parents

Handling tantrums gracefully requires patience, which can be challenging if you're feeling stressed or exhausted. Prioritize your own well-being to maintain emotional resilience.

CHAPTER SEVEN

THE ROLE OF PLAY IN EARLY CHILDHOOD DEVELOPMENT: ENCOURAGING CREATIVITY

Play is often considered a vital component of early childhood development, providing children with the opportunity to explore, learn and develop important cognitive, social, emotional and physical skills. Through play, children can interact with their environment, discover new concepts and enhance their creativity, laying the foundation for a lifetime of learning and growth. In early childhood, the role of play goes beyond simple entertainment it serves as a fundamental tool that nurtures creativity, problem-solving and social abilities, while fostering emotional well-being and cognitive development.

Cognitive Development through Play

One of the most significant benefits of play in early

childhood is its contribution to cognitive development. During play, children are exposed to a variety of concepts such as cause and effect, categorization, and symbolic thinking, all of which are essential for learning. For example, when children play with building blocks, they develop spatial awareness, understanding shapes and learning how objects interact with one another. Such activities require children to think critically, make decisions and experiment with different ways of structuring their play, all of which enhance their problem-solving abilities.

Furthermore, imaginative play encourages children to engage in symbolic thinking. For example, when a child pretends a stick is a sword or a box is a spaceship, they are using their imagination to transform ordinary objects into representations of something entirely different. This form of play is instrumental in fostering abstract thinking, which is crucial for understanding more complex ideas as children grow older.

Additionally, play often involves following rules and guidelines, which teaches children how to focus, follow instructions and work within a set structure. Games with rules, such as board games or card games, require children to apply logic, understand patterns and practice memory all critical components of cognitive development.

Encouraging Creativity through Play

Creativity is another key aspect that is nurtured through play, and it plays an essential role in a child's development. Creative play allows children to express themselves, solve problems in unique ways, and explore new ideas. Engaging in art activities such as drawing, painting and crafting helps children experiment with colors, shapes and textures, while also improving fine motor skills and hand-eye coordination. When children have the freedom to explore these artistic outlets, they begin to develop a sense of individuality and autonomy.

Moreover, pretend play, also known as dramatic play, enables children to act out scenarios that encourage them to think outside the box. They may take on the roles of various characters, such as a doctor, teacher, or parent, and through these experiences, they learn to see the world from different perspectives. This type of imaginative play also boosts creativity by allowing children to invent stories, come up with solutions to problems, and explore different aspects of social and emotional roles in a safe environment.

Play-based learning often prioritizes hands-on experiences, encouraging children to interact with materials and objects that inspire creativity. For instance, playing with clay, building models or engaging in sensory play with different textures can stimulate creativity by giving children the opportunity to manipulate the physical world and experiment with their surroundings. These activities teach children that there are multiple ways to solve problems, and sometimes, there is no single "right" answer—only different possibilities.

Social and Emotional Growth through Play

In addition to cognitive and creative development, play plays a critical role in fostering emotional and social growth. Children's early social interactions during play help them develop essential social skills, including cooperation, communication and conflict resolution. Whether playing with peers or adults, children learn how to take turns, share resources, negotiate with others and respect different viewpoints. These social interactions set the stage for later social competence, making children more adept at forming positive relationships in the future.

Role-playing games are particularly helpful in developing empathy, as they require children to step into the shoes of others. For example, when a child plays "house," they may take on the role of a parent, learning to care for others, or they may pretend to be a teacher, practicing leadership skills. These experiences help children understand the emotions and perspectives of others, which is crucial for developing emotional intelligence. Through play, children practice expressing their feelings and recognizing those of others, an important skill for navigating social relationships.

Additionally, play provides a safe environment for children to explore their emotions and develop coping mechanisms. It offers them a space to express joy, frustration, or sadness in a way that is both constructive and non-threatening. For instance, when children are playing a game and lose, they may experience disappointment. However, through supportive play interactions with adults or peers, they learn how to manage frustration, practice resilience, and eventually gain a sense of achievement when they overcome obstacles.

Physical Development through Play

Physical play is another important aspect of early childhood development. Active play, which involves running, jumping, climbing and other physical activities, is essential for the development of gross motor skills. These activities not only build strength, coordination, and balance but also contribute to the overall physical health of children. Engaging in physical play also helps children improve their stamina and endurance, while fostering an early love for physical activity that can contribute to healthy habits throughout life.

Fine motor skills, which involve smaller, more precise movements, are also developed through play. Activities such as drawing, cutting with scissors, manipulating small objects, or assembling puzzles all contribute to fine motor development, enabling children to refine their dexterity and hand-eye coordination. These skills are essential for a wide range of daily tasks, such as writing, dressing and feeding themselves.

The Role of Play in Early Education

Educators recognize that play is an effective teaching tool that fosters active learning. Many early childhood education programs incorporate play-based learning into their curricula because it allows children to learn in a natural, engaging, and hands-on way. By creating an environment that encourages exploration and imagination, teachers provide children with the opportunity to discover new concepts, practice new skills and deepen their understanding of the world around them.

Play-based learning supports a child's intrinsic motivation to learn, as it taps into their curiosity and sense of wonder. Rather than forcing children to absorb information in a traditional, structured manner, play encourages them to ask questions, explore ideas and experiment with different solutions. As such, it nurtures a lifelong love of learning that transcends formal education settings.

Play is a cornerstone of early childhood development, encouraging creativity, cognitive growth, emotional intelligence and social skills. Through various forms of play, children have the freedom to explore their world, develop new ideas and refine their abilities in a fun and engaging way. Play-based learning helps children build essential skills that will serve them throughout their lives. Therefore, it is crucial for parents, caregivers and educators to create environments that encourage and support meaningful play, ensuring that children have the best possible start in their developmental journey.

CHAPTER EIGTH

ESTABLISHING ROUTINES: HOW STRUCTURE SHAPES A CHILD'S CONFIDENCE AND SECURITY

Establishing routines is an essential aspect of child development, playing a crucial role in shaping a child's confidence, emotional security and overall well-being. Children thrive in structured environments where expectations are clear and consistency is a fundamental part of their daily lives. When routines are thoughtfully established, they offer a sense of safety and predictability, both of which are key to fostering a healthy, confident and emotionally resilient child. This article will explore how routines contribute to a child's confidence and security, highlighting the psychological, emotional and developmental benefits of structure in their lives.

The Importance of Predictability and Consistency

One of the core aspects of establishing routines is the sense of predictability they create for children. From waking up to going to bed, children rely on a predictable flow of activities to understand what is expected of them at any given time. For example, a routine that includes consistent mealtimes, playtimes, nap times and bedtime provides children with clear signals about the passage of time and the activities they can expect.

When children know what to expect, they can mentally prepare for transitions, reducing feelings of anxiety and uncertainty. This predictability can be especially comforting for younger children or those who are prone to anxiety. Knowing that after breakfast, for instance, there will be a time for play, then a story, and finally, a nap, helps them anticipate what's coming next. This structure reduces stress, as children no longer have to wonder what happens next or worry about unexpected disruptions.

Consistency is equally important in ensuring that these routines are followed with minimal variation. The more consistently routines are applied, the more effective they are in helping children feel secure. This consistency is not only about the timing of activities but also about reinforcing behaviors and expectations. When a child knows that their parents or caregivers will consistently respond in a certain way to their needs whether it's a comforting hug at bedtime or a regular afternoon snack—they begin to trust the environment around them. This trust builds a foundation for emotional security, enabling the child to feel confident in their ability to navigate the world.

Structure and Emotional Regulation

Routines provide more than just predictability; they also offer structure that helps children develop emotional regulation. Emotional regulation is the ability to manage one's emotions, particularly in stressful or challenging situations, and it is a vital life skill. By following a structured routine, children learn to recognize and manage their emotional responses.

For instance, having a set routine for bedtime, including winding down activities such as reading or listening to soft music, helps children transition from the excitement of the day to the calmness of the evening. This structured approach allows children to regulate their emotions, preparing their bodies and minds for rest. Over time, children who are given opportunities to practice emotional regulation within a structured routine become better equipped to handle emotional challenges in other areas of life.

Additionally, when children understand that their routine allows for time to play, socialize, and engage with others, they experience a sense of control over their emotional world. They can look forward to certain activities, creating a balance between responsibilities and relaxation. This equilibrium helps children feel more in control of their emotions and less overwhelmed by the fluctuations of daily life.

Routines Foster Confidence

Confidence is intricately linked to a child's ability to predict and control their environment. A child who feels that they are in a predictable and structured environment is more likely to feel secure and capable of handling the challenges they encounter. When children know what is expected of them, they are more likely to approach each task with a sense of competence.

For example, if a child has a routine that includes designated times for homework, they become accustomed to the idea that academic tasks are a regular part of their day. Over time, this helps them develop a sense of mastery over their work, which contributes to self-confidence. Knowing that they can handle daily responsibilities, such as getting dressed or tidying up their toys, strengthens a child's sense of accomplishment and competence.

Moreover, routines allow children to feel more independent as they grow older. The more children are given the opportunity to follow a routine on their own, the more they develop a sense of autonomy. For instance, a child may learn to brush their teeth as part of their morning routine, gradually becoming more confident in their ability to care for themselves. Autonomy within the context of a structured routine fosters self-esteem and encourages children to take on new challenges with confidence.

Routines and Behavioral Expectations

Clear routines help children develop an understanding of behavioral expectations. When routines are reinforced with consistent rules and consequences, children learn about boundaries and what is acceptable behavior. A structured routine, such as one that includes time for chores or family interactions, teaches children the importance of responsibility, cooperation and respect for others.

This aspect of structure is particularly important in the development of social skills. A child who follows a routine that includes time for social interaction, such as playdates or family meals, learns how to engage with others in a respectful and meaningful way. The predictability of these interactions allows children to feel secure in their relationships, knowing what to expect and how to behave.

In contrast, children who lack routine may struggle with understanding behavioral expectations, as they may not have consistent opportunities to practice these skills. A lack of routine can lead to confusion or frustration, as children may not know how to navigate different social situations or regulate their emotions effectively.

The Role of Routines in Developing Healthy Habits

Establishing a routine from an early age also helps children develop healthy habits. Whether it's eating nutritious meals, exercising, or practicing good hygiene, routines provide a framework for children to adopt behaviors that will serve them well throughout their lives. A routine that includes regular meal times encourages children to eat at consistent intervals, promoting healthy digestion and nutrition. Similarly, regular physical activity, such as an after-school routine of outdoor play or exercise, contributes to physical health and well-being.

Good sleep hygiene is another example of how routines promote healthy habits. A child who follows a consistent bedtime routine, such as winding down with a bath and a bedtime story, is more likely to establish healthy sleep patterns. These positive habits contribute to a child's physical health, emotional regulation and overall confidence in their ability to manage their daily life.

Establishing routines is a powerful tool for fostering a child's confidence and security. Through predictable structures, children learn to regulate their emotions, develop independence and gain the confidence to navigate the world.

Middle Childhood (6-12 Years)

CHAPTER NINE

FOSTERING INDEPENDENCE: ALLOWING YOUR CHILD TO EXPLORE AND GROW SAFELY

Fostering independence in children is a crucial part of their development, as it helps them build confidence, develop problem-solving skills and gain a sense of autonomy. Allowing a child to explore and grow safely is not just about giving them the freedom to act on their own but also ensuring they do so in a supportive and safe environment. This balance between independence and safety is essential for raising children who are capable, responsible and resilient.

The Importance of Independence

Independence is an essential life skill that children must learn to succeed both in childhood and as adults. When children are encouraged to make decisions on their own, they learn to trust their abilities and develop a sense of self-reliance. These skills are critical for emotional regulation and social competence. Additionally, fostering independence helps children understand that they are responsible for their actions and the consequences that follow.

From a young age, children start to explore their environment. They begin by taking small steps, such as crawling or walking, before advancing to more complex tasks like problem-solving, making decisions and interacting with others. As children mature, their need for independence grows, and parents must find ways to support them without stifling their growth. This involves offering opportunities for exploration while maintaining a protective and guiding role.

Setting the Stage for Safe Exploration

For children to explore and grow, they must first feel safe. Creating an environment that promotes both safety and autonomy is key. Parents can set boundaries and guidelines while allowing space for children to make their own choices. For example, a child may want to ride a bike independently; instead of simply denying the request out of fear, parents can provide a safe route and proper safety equipment, such as a helmet and pads, while giving the child the freedom to enjoy the activity.

In the early stages of childhood, safety often means controlling the environment, such as childproofing the house and keeping dangerous objects out of reach. As children grow, the focus shifts from controlling their environment to teaching them about safety and consequences. For example, parents can explain the importance of wearing a seatbelt, looking both ways before crossing the street, and following safety rules at school or in public spaces. By doing so, children learn that independence comes with responsibility.

Encouraging Age-Appropriate Risks

Independence isn't just about providing opportunities for children to make decisions; it also involves encouraging them to take age-appropriate risks. Taking risks helps children understand their limitations, build resilience, and develop problem-solving skills. The key is to ensure the risks are manageable and safe. Allowing children to experience failure is an important part of the learning process, as it teaches them how to cope with disappointment and how to persevere.

For example, if a child is learning how to ride a bike, they may fall a few times before they master the skill. While the experience may be uncomfortable, it is a valuable lesson in persistence. If parents are overly cautious and prevent their child from taking risks, they may limit the child's growth and prevent them from learning how to handle challenges.

Parents can help children learn how to assess risks and make informed decisions. One way to do this is by asking questions that prompt the child to think critically about their choices. For instance, if a child wants to go to a friend's house, a parent might ask, "How will you get there?" or "What will you do if you need help?" These questions encourage children to consider the logistics and potential challenges of the situation, which helps them develop the skills needed for independent decision-making.

Gradual Increase in Responsibility

As children grow, they should be given progressively more responsibility in areas like chores, schoolwork, and personal care. Parents should tailor these responsibilities to the child's age and abilities, gradually increasing the level of complexity. For example, a toddler might begin by putting away toys, while an older child might take on the responsibility of preparing a simple meal or managing their own homework schedule.

This incremental approach to responsibility helps children build self-confidence and understand that they are capable of handling tasks on their own. It also fosters a sense of accomplishment and pride in their abilities. Additionally, when children are given responsibilities, they learn the importance of time management and organization, which are vital skills in both academic and personal life.

Allowing children to make mistakes as they take on new responsibilities is also important. Parents should provide support when necessary, but they should avoid stepping in too quickly to fix problems. This gives children the opportunity to learn from their mistakes, which is a critical aspect of growing up.

The Role of Communication and Guidance

While fostering independence is crucial, it is important for parents to maintain open communication with their children. This involves listening to their thoughts, concerns and ideas, and offering guidance when needed. Children need to feel that they can approach their parents for advice or support, but they should also know that they have the freedom to make their own choices.

One way to maintain a balance between independence and guidance is through regular family discussions. These discussions allow children to express their feelings and thoughts in a safe, open environment. Parents can use these conversations to reinforce safety rules, share personal experiences, and offer advice without imposing their own preferences.

Guidance can also involve setting clear expectations and providing positive reinforcement. When children make good choices, parents can acknowledge their success, which reinforces their sense of competence and independence. Encouragement and praise go a long way in boosting a child's confidence and motivating them to take on new challenges.

The Impact on Future Growth

The ability to explore and grow independently is vital not only during childhood but also in preparing for adulthood. Children who are allowed to make decisions, take risks and experience consequences develop the skills they need to thrive in life. They are more likely to be self-sufficient, resilient and capable of handling the challenges that come with adulthood. By fostering independence in a safe and supportive environment, parents lay the foundation for their children to grow into confident, responsible individuals.

In conclusion, fostering independence involves a delicate balance of freedom and safety. By allowing children to explore and grow on their own, parents help them build self-confidence, problem-solving skills and emotional resilience. With appropriate guidance, age-appropriate risks and increasing responsibilities, children can develop the skills needed to navigate the world with autonomy and confidence. The goal is not to control every aspect of a child's life but to give them the tools and opportunities to learn and grow in a safe, nurturing environment.

CHAPTER TEN

INSTILLING VALUES AND MORALS: TEACHING KINDNESS, RESPONSIBILITY AND RESPECT

Instilling values and morals in children is a fundamental aspect of parenting and education, as it shapes the future behavior, decision-making, and character of young individuals. Values like kindness, responsibility and respect are not only essential in fostering a healthy and harmonious society, but they also help children build strong interpersonal relationships, navigate challenges and contribute positively to their communities. Teaching these values requires intentional guidance, modeling by adults and creating environments where these qualities are reinforced regularly. In this essay, we will explore the importance of instilling kindness, responsibility, and respect in children, along with strategies for nurturing these values effectively.

Kindness: The Foundation of Positive Social Interaction

Kindness is one of the most universally cherished virtues, playing a crucial role in how individuals interact with one another. It involves showing empathy, compassion and consideration for the feelings and needs of others. Teaching children to be kind encourages them to look beyond their own needs and develop the ability to care for others, which is essential for creating supportive and cooperative relationships.

The role of kindness in a child's development extends beyond just social interactions; it fosters emotional intelligence and self-awareness. A child who practices kindness learns to be more in tune with the emotional states of others, which helps build stronger bonds with peers and adults alike. Research suggests that children who engage in acts of kindness also experience emotional benefits, such as increased feelings of happiness and self-esteem.

Parents and educators can instill kindness in children by providing opportunities for them to engage in acts of empathy, such as helping a classmate with a task or comforting a friend who is upset. Modeling kind behavior is also key. Children learn by observing the actions of adults, so when parents demonstrate kindness in their everyday interactions whether it's helping a neighbor, listening attentively or expressing gratitude they set a powerful example for their children to follow.

Moreover, children should be encouraged to appreciate the value of small acts of kindness. A simple "thank you," offering a compliment, or sharing with others are all forms of kindness that children can easily practice. Positive reinforcement from adults, such as praise for these acts, reinforces the behavior and makes kindness feel rewarding.

Responsibility: Empowering Children to Take Ownership

Responsibility is an essential value that helps children develop a sense of accountability for their actions, decisions, and commitments. It is closely tied to a child's sense of self-efficacy and personal development, teaching them to understand that their actions have consequences, both positive and negative. By instilling responsibility, parents and educators help children grow into self-reliant individuals who are capable of managing their own affairs and contributing to the greater good.

Teaching responsibility starts with allowing children to take ownership of age-appropriate tasks. For younger children, this might mean taking responsibility for their belongings, such as putting away toys or cleaning up after themselves. As children grow, responsibilities can evolve to include chores, schoolwork, and even caring for pets or siblings. In all cases, children should be encouraged to follow through on their commitments. Failure to meet responsibilities should be met with appropriate consequences, not punishment, but a learning experience to help them understand the importance of accountability.

An important aspect of teaching responsibility is promoting a growth mindset encouraging children to believe that their efforts lead to success and that mistakes are opportunities to learn and grow. This attitude helps children take responsibility for their actions without fear of failure, encouraging them to try again after setbacks and to own their successes with humility.

It is also important to teach children the value of time management and the importance of setting priorities. These lessons can be imparted by helping children create schedules or break down larger tasks into manageable steps. When children are taught how to plan, set goals, and meet deadlines, they are learning the practical aspects of responsibility that will serve them well into adulthood.

Respect: Building a Foundation for Healthy Relationships

Respect is a cornerstone of healthy relationships, and it is critical in ensuring that individuals treat each other with dignity, fairness and consideration. Respect for others and oneself is vital for navigating personal, social, and professional environments. In early childhood, respect is learned through understanding boundaries, showing appreciation for the differences of others and acknowledging the value of each individual.

Teaching respect involves both setting clear boundaries and demonstrating how respect looks in action. Children should understand the importance of listening to others, considering other people's perspectives, and being polite in their interactions. Practicing respectful behavior starts with understanding the concept of fairness and justice—treating others as they would like to be treated. This golden rule, commonly taught in childhood, serves as a powerful guide for respectful behavior.

A child who is taught respect learns to honor the feelings, rights, and beliefs of others, even if they differ from their own. It also involves teaching children how to resolve conflicts in a respectful way. Instead of resorting to aggression or withdrawing, children should learn to express their feelings calmly, listen to the views of others and find mutually agreeable solutions to problems.

Just as with kindness and responsibility, respect is best taught by modeling it. When parents or educators demonstrate respect for others, children are more likely to adopt this behavior. Respecting a child's own rights and autonomy is also a key part of the process. When children are treated with respect, they internalize the value and apply it to their relationships with others.

Additionally, teaching children to respect their own

bodies and minds is essential for their well-being. Self -respect encourages children to make healthy decisions, set boundaries, and avoid situations where they might feel uncomfortable or unsafe. It also lays the foundation for fostering self-confidence and independence.

The Lasting Impact of Instilling Values

Instilling values like kindness, responsibility and respect in children sets them on a path to becoming compassionate, dependable and considerate adults. These values create a strong foundation for personal growth and they foster positive, productive relationships. Parents, educators and caregivers all have critical roles in nurturing these virtues by modeling the behaviors they wish to instill, providing consistent reinforcement, and creating environments where these values can thrive. As children internalize these values, they will be better equipped to navigate life's challenges, contribute to society and lead with empathy, integrity and respect for others.

CHAPTER ELEVEN

HELPING YOUR CHILD DEVELOP HEALTHY
FRIENDSHIPS: NAVIGATING PEER RELATIONSHIPS

Friendship plays an integral role in a child's emotional, social and cognitive development. From early childhood to adolescence, friendships offer children opportunities to explore their identity, practice social skills, and learn about empathy, trust and conflict resolution. However, navigating peer relationships can be challenging, especially as children grow and their social environments become more complex. Parents play a vital role in guiding their children through this developmental phase, helping them form healthy friendships and manage the inevitable ups and downs of peer interactions.

The Importance of Healthy Friendships

Healthy friendships contribute significantly to a child's well-being. They provide emotional support, reduce feelings of loneliness and enhance self-esteem.

Friendships also help children develop essential life skills such as effective communication, cooperation, problem-solving and emotional regulation. A study by the American Psychological Association (APA) emphasizes that peer relationships during childhood influence mental health, social functioning and even academic performance. Positive peer interactions enable children to feel accepted, build a sense of belonging, and develop a strong sense of self.

On the other hand, unhealthy friendships or peer rejection can lead to issues such as social anxiety, bullying and low self-esteem. It is crucial for parents to help children understand what constitutes a healthy friendship, how to choose good friends, and how to handle conflicts that may arise in relationships.

KEY STRATEGIES FOR SUPPORTING HEALTHY FRIENDSHIPS

1. Fostering Emotional Intelligence

Emotional intelligence (EI) is the ability to recognize, understand and manage emotions in oneself and others. Children with high EI are more likely to navigate peer relationships successfully. Parents can foster EI by teaching children how to express their feelings appropriately, recognize the emotions of others and empathize with peers. Encouraging children to label their emotions, such as saying "I feel sad" or "I'm angry," helps them communicate more effectively with friends and peers.

Parents can model empathetic behaviors by responding to their child's emotions with care and understanding, and by encouraging children to do the same with others. For example, teaching children to listen to their friends' problems and offering support, rather than jumping to solutions or dismissing feelings, helps them form deeper, more meaningful friendships.

2. Encouraging Open Communication

Open communication is the foundation of any strong relationship. Children need to feel comfortable talking about their friendships, whether they're feeling happy or facing challenges with their peers. Parents should create an environment where their children feel safe to share their experiences. This requires being an active listener, avoiding judgment and showing empathy when discussing social situations.

Parents should ask open-ended questions like, "How did you feel when you played with your friend today?" or "What did you do when you disagreed with someone?" These questions give children the opportunity to express their thoughts and feelings, and allow parents to provide guidance when necessary.

In addition, parents can teach their children the importance of clear communication with their friends. Encouraging children to express their needs, feelings, and boundaries respectfully can prevent misunderstandings and help resolve conflicts before they escalate.

3. Teaching Social Skills

Social skills are crucial for forming healthy friendships. Children need to learn how to initiate conversations, ask questions, make eye contact, take turns in conversations and share. Parents can role-play these scenarios at home to give children the tools they need to engage with peers in a positive way. For example, parents can model how to introduce oneself or how to join a group activity.

It's also important to teach children how to resolve conflicts. Disagreements are a normal part of any friendship, but learning how to handle them with maturity is essential. Parents can encourage their children to think about how their words or actions might affect others and guide them in finding peaceful solutions. Teaching children to apologize when necessary, take responsibility for their actions, and forgive others when appropriate builds resilience and emotional intelligence.

4. Setting Boundaries and Recognizing Red Flags

While it's important to encourage children to form relationships, parents must also teach them about setting healthy boundaries. Children need to understand that they have the right to say "no" when something doesn't feel right, whether it's being pressured into doing something they're uncomfortable with or being treated unfairly.

Parents should talk to their children about recognizing red flags in friendships, such as when a friend is overly controlling, mean-spirited, or dishonest. Children must be taught how to identify and navigate toxic relationships, which may require stepping away from certain individuals who are not treating them with respect.

5. Providing Opportunities for Peer Interaction

For children to develop friendships, they need opportunities to interact with their peers in a variety of settings. Parents can encourage participation in extracurricular activities, sports and social events where children can meet new friends and engage in different types of group interactions. By exposing children to diverse social settings, they can learn how to relate to a variety of personalities and develop empathy for others.

Parents can also host playdates or small group gatherings to help their children connect with others outside of school or formal settings. These informal interactions allow children to practice socializing in a more relaxed environment, which can help ease the pressures that come with large group settings.

6. Guiding Children Through Friendship Challenges

Friendships aren't always smooth sailing. Conflicts, misunderstandings, and even bullying may occur. When children face difficulties in their friendships, parents can help them process these emotions and guide them in resolving issues. It's essential for parents to listen carefully to their child's perspective, validate their feelings, and help them think through potential solutions.

If a child is being bullied or excluded, it's crucial for parents to take appropriate action. They should encourage their child to stand up for themselves, seek support from a trusted adult, and report any incidents of bullying. In more severe cases, parents may need to intervene by contacting school officials or seeking professional counseling.

Helping your child develop healthy friendships is a critical aspect of their overall development. By fostering emotional intelligence, encouraging open communication, teaching social skills and providing opportunities for positive peer interactions, parents can play a pivotal role in guiding their children through the complexities of friendship. Additionally, equipping children with the skills to set boundaries, recognize unhealthy friendships and handle conflicts empowers them to build lasting, meaningful relationships.

Ultimately, healthy friendships lay the foundation for a child's emotional well-being, resilience, and success in navigating the social challenges of life.

CHAPTER TWELVE

THE IMPORTANCE OF ACADEMIC SUPPORT: ENCOURAGING A LOVE FOR LEARNING WITHOUT PRESSURE

In the rapidly evolving world of education, the role of academic support has become increasingly important. It goes beyond simply aiding students in achieving high grades. Instead, academic support is about creating a nurturing environment where students feel encouraged to explore, develop critical thinking skills, and find joy in learning, all while reducing the often-overwhelming pressures associated with academic achievement. This support is essential not only for academic success but for the overall well-being and emotional growth of students.

The Foundation of Academic Support

Academic support can take many forms, including personalized tutoring, peer mentoring, online resources, and after-school programs. It can also be as simple as fostering an open, understanding relationship between students and teachers. The goal of academic support is to ensure that students have the tools and guidance they need to succeed at their own pace, with a focus on both short-term performance and long-term intellectual growth.

However, what truly sets effective academic support apart is its ability to create a balanced atmosphere where students feel safe to express their struggles and curiosities. The support they receive is not solely aimed at improving grades but at helping them develop a genuine interest in the subjects they are learning. By removing the fear of failure and emphasizing the value of effort and persistence, students are more likely to adopt a love for learning that can last a lifetime.

The Role of Teachers and Educators

Teachers play a critical role in fostering an environment of academic support. They are not only responsible for teaching the curriculum but also for recognizing when a student is struggling. Through effective academic support, teachers can create tailored strategies to address the individual needs of their students. Whether a student needs extra help with reading comprehension, mathematical concepts or developing strong study habits, personalized support allows teachers to meet the student at their level, making learning more accessible and less intimidating.

Moreover, teachers who are sensitive to students' emotional and intellectual needs can guide them in a way that nurtures their self-confidence. A teacher who encourages questions, praises efforts over results and shows patience can greatly reduce academic anxiety. This atmosphere encourages students to seek help without the fear of judgment, helping them develop a mindset that values growth over perfection.

Academic Support Beyond the Classroom

While teachers are at the forefront of academic support, there are other forms of assistance that can provide a broader and more holistic approach to a student's education. Peer tutoring, for example, is an effective way of providing academic support in a non-threatening environment. Often, students feel more comfortable asking questions and seeking help from their peers because there is less fear of judgment. Peer tutors can offer explanations in a more relatable way, fostering a sense of camaraderie and reinforcing the idea that learning is a collaborative process rather than a solitary endeavor.

Furthermore, after-school programs and online tutoring platforms allow students to access support outside of regular classroom hours. These programs offer an opportunity for students to explore subjects in more depth, work on specific areas of weakness or even explore areas of interest that may not be covered in the standard curriculum. Such support mechanisms ensure that academic assistance is available when students need it most, without the constraints of classroom time.

Encouraging a Love for Learning Without Pressure

One of the most significant advantages of academic support is its ability to remove pressure from the learning process. In many educational systems, there is a heavy emphasis on performance and grades, leading students to view learning as a means to an end rather than as an enjoyable and lifelong pursuit. This pressure can result in burnout, disengagement, and a lack of intrinsic motivation.

Academic support provides a counterbalance to this by shifting the focus away from grades and placing it on the process of learning itself. When students receive encouragement, constructive feedback, and the chance to explore subjects in an engaging way, they are more likely to develop an intrinsic love for learning. They begin to view challenges as opportunities for growth rather than obstacles to success. When failure is seen not as a sign of incompetence but as a part of the learning process, students are more likely to take risks and engage more deeply with the material.

Moreover, when students are encouraged to pursue learning without the weight of external pressure, they can develop skills beyond memorization. They are more likely to become critical thinkers, problem-solvers and independent learners. These skills are invaluable not only in academics but in life, where the ability to learn continuously and adapt is essential.

Supporting Emotional and Mental Health

The importance of academic support also extends to students' emotional and mental well-being. Academic pressure can often lead to stress, anxiety and a sense of inadequacy, particularly when students struggle to meet high expectations. For many, the idea of falling behind or not living up to their potential can feel overwhelming. This is where academic support systems that emphasize encouragement, rather than just achievement, can make a profound difference.

By providing emotional support alongside academic help, students can build resilience and develop coping strategies for managing stress. When they are offered the reassurance that they are capable of improving with effort and time, they gain a sense of control over their learning process. This positive reinforcement, coupled with a reduction in pressure, helps students feel empowered and more engaged in their academic journey.

Building Lifelong Learners

In the long term, academic support fosters a mindset that is crucial for success in both education and life: the mindset of a lifelong learner. When students are given the tools and confidence to learn without fear of failure, they are more likely to continue seeking knowledge and personal growth as they mature. This mindset not only benefits students in their academic careers but also in their personal and professional lives, as they become more adaptable, curious and proactive.

The importance of academic support cannot be overstated. It is not just about helping students succeed in their exams but about fostering a love for learning that will serve them for the rest of their lives. By creating an environment that encourages intellectual exploration, supports emotional well-being and removes the pressure to constantly perform, academic support can transform students' attitudes toward learning. It provides them with the tools, confidence and motivation to succeed in both their education and life, ensuring they can navigate the challenges of the future with curiosity and resilience.

CHAPTER THIRTEEN

NAVIGATING TEEN INDEPENDENCE: STRIKING THE BALANCE BETWEEN FREEDOM AND BOUNDARIES

Adolescence is a time of significant change, both physically and emotionally. As teenagers transition from childhood to adulthood, they begin to seek more independence and autonomy. This developmental stage can be both exhilarating and challenging for teens and their parents alike. Parents often find themselves caught between fostering their child's growing need for freedom and providing appropriate guidance and boundaries. The key to navigating this phase is striking a delicate balance between granting independence and maintaining boundaries that ensure safety, responsibility and healthy development.

The Importance of Teen Independence

Teenagers crave independence as part of their psychological and emotional growth. They are beginning to form their own identities, separate from their families, and they desire to make decisions about their lives, relationships and future. According to developmental psychology, this quest for autonomy is an essential part of becoming an independent adult. Teen independence is also linked to developing self-confidence, decision-making skills and a sense of responsibility.

As teens start to push against their parents' rules, it is important for both parties to recognize that this is a natural and necessary part of development. Research suggests that fostering independence helps teenagers build the resilience they will need to navigate the adult world. However, the degree of freedom granted must be matched with guidance to help teens make sound decisions and learn from their mistakes.

The Role of Boundaries in Teen Development

While granting teens independence is essential, boundaries remain crucial. Boundaries provide structure and help teens understand the limits of acceptable behavior. They also protect teens from harm and guide them in making informed choices. Setting appropriate boundaries enables parents to teach their children essential life skills such as time management, financial responsibility and respectful relationships. It also ensures that teens don't engage in risky behaviors that may have lasting consequences, such as substance abuse, unsafe sexual activity, or poor academic performance.

Boundaries can take various forms, from curfews and guidelines for social media use to rules surrounding schoolwork and household responsibilities. These rules should be communicated clearly and consistently, with the understanding that they are not meant to control, but to guide and protect. Without clear boundaries, teens may struggle with impulse control and decision-making, or feel overwhelmed by the lack of structure, which can lead to anxiety or poor choices.

Finding the Right Balance

The challenge lies in striking the right balance between independence and boundaries. Here are some strategies that can help parents find this balance:

1. Open Communication: Communication is the cornerstone of any healthy relationship, and this holds especially true for the parent-teen dynamic. Parents must encourage open and honest discussions with their teenagers, allowing them to voice their opinions, concerns, and desires for independence. Teens should feel heard and understood, and their perspectives should be validated. At the same time, parents should assertively share their values and reasoning behind the rules they set, helping teens understand that boundaries are not arbitrary but are in place to help them grow and stay safe.

2. Gradual Increase in Responsibility: One effective way to balance freedom and boundaries is to grant teens more responsibility over time. As they demonstrate maturity and sound judgment, they should be

given more opportunities to make decisions and manage their own lives. For example, a teen might start by having a curfew that gradually extends as they prove they can be trusted to follow the rules. Likewise, parents might start giving their teens more control over their finances or school decisions as they grow older.

3. Mutual Respect and Trust: Building a foundation of mutual respect is essential. Parents must respect their teens' growing need for independence and trust them to make the right choices, while still offering guidance when needed. This two-way respect is vital for maintaining a positive relationship and for preventing the friction that often arises during the teen years. When teens feel trusted and respected, they are more likely to reciprocate by adhering to boundaries and rules.

4. Flexibility and Adaptability: Flexibility is key in navigating teen independence. Each adolescent is unique, with different needs and levels of maturity. What works for one teen may not work for another. Parents should be prepared to adapt their approach to their child's individual temperament, preferences and experiences. It's also important to be open to modifying boundaries when appropriate, especially when teens demonstrate growth and maturity.

5. Modeling Positive Behavior: Teenagers often

learn by observing the behavior of their parents. By modeling responsible decision-making, emotional regulation, and healthy relationships, parents can set an example for their children. For instance, if a parent demonstrates a strong work ethic, their teen is likely to adopt similar habits. Additionally, if parents show respect for others' boundaries, teens are more likely to understand the importance of respecting their own limits and those of others.

6. Consequences and Accountability: Along with setting boundaries, it is important to establish consequences for violating rules. These consequences should be fair, consistent and appropriate for the behavior in question. When teens understand that their actions have consequences, they are more likely to make responsible choices. Importantly, consequences should also be used as opportunities for learning, not as a means of punishment. Instead of focusing solely on the negative aspects of misbehavior, parents can use it as a teaching moment to help their teens understand the impact of their actions and learn from their mistakes.

The Importance of Emotional Support

Even as teens seek more independence, they still need emotional support from their parents.

Adolescence can be an emotionally turbulent time, and teens may face challenges related to their self-esteem, peer relationships and academic pressures. While they may resist overt expressions of affection, they still need reassurance and emotional stability from their families. Parents should continue to provide encouragement, celebrate their achievements and offer comfort during difficult times.

Navigating the transition from dependence to independence during the teen years is a delicate balance that requires careful attention and understanding. By fostering open communication, granting increasing levels of responsibility, maintaining clear boundaries and providing emotional support, parents can help their teens develop into responsible, self-confident young adults. Striking the right balance between freedom and boundaries allows teens to explore their independence while ensuring they have the guidance and structure needed to thrive in the complex world around them.

CHAPTER FOURTEEN

UNDERSTANDING TEEN EMOTIONS: HOW TO SUPPORT YOUR CHILD THROUGH ADOLESCENCE

Adolescence is a transformative period in life marked by rapid physical, emotional and social changes. During this time, teens experience significant shifts in their feelings, thoughts and behaviors, which can sometimes be confusing and challenging for both them and their parents. Understanding these emotional changes is crucial for offering the right support and fostering a healthy, trusting relationship between parents and their teenage children. In this article, we will explore the nature of teen emotions, the factors influencing them and practical ways parents can support their child during this critical developmental stage.

The Emotional Landscape of Adolescence

The teenage years are often associated with mood swings, heightened emotional reactions and an overall sense of unpredictability. These emotional fluctuations are due to several factors, including hormonal changes, brain development and the quest for identity. Understanding the biological underpinnings of adolescence can help parents make sense of their child's emotional responses.

1. Hormonal Changes: The surge in hormones such as estrogen and testosterone that occurs during puberty plays a significant role in the intensity of a teen's emotions. These hormonal fluctuations can cause emotional extremes, from extreme happiness to sudden bouts of anger or sadness, often with little warning. As their bodies and brains adjust to these hormonal shifts, teenagers may experience intense feelings they are still learning how to manage and express.

2. Brain Development: The adolescent brain undergoes significant development, particularly in areas related to decision-making, emotional regulation, and social behavior. The prefrontal cortex, responsible for reasoning and impulse control, is not fully developed during the teenage years, which explains some of the rash decisions and impulsive behaviors that teens sometimes exhibit. On the other hand, the limbic system, the part of the brain responsible

for emotions, is highly active during this stage, which can lead to heightened emotional responses.

3. Search for Identity: Adolescence is also a time of self-discovery and identity formation. Teens are working hard to establish who they are, what they believe and where they fit in the world. This can lead to internal conflict, confusion, and emotional turmoil. Teens often question their values, their role in their family and peer groups, and their place in society, which can make them feel vulnerable and misunderstood.

4. Social and Peer Influence: Peer relationships become central during adolescence. Teens often place great importance on fitting in and being accepted by their peers, which can influence their emotional state. The need for social validation can cause teens to feel anxious, lonely, or excluded, especially if they are struggling with friendships or facing peer pressure. This social component of adolescence makes teens highly sensitive to their interactions with others and can amplify emotional reactions.

Recognizing Emotional Struggles

One of the challenges for parents during adolescence is recognizing when emotional struggles are a normal part of growing up versus when they may signal a deeper issue. Teenagers may express their emotions in different ways than younger children, and these expressions can sometimes be difficult to decipher.

1. Mood Swings and Irritability: While some mood swings are expected, especially during the early teenage years, parents should be attuned to persistent changes in their child's mood. If a teen is frequently irritable, withdrawn, or overly emotional for an extended period, it could be a sign of anxiety, depression, or another underlying issue.
2. Withdrawal and Isolation: A certain degree of independence is typical as teens begin to distance themselves from their parents to develop their own identities. However, if a teen becomes excessively isolated, refusing to engage in family activities, or expressing a desire to cut off contact with friends or family, it could signal depression or other emotional struggles.
3. Changes in Behavior or Academic Performance: A sudden drop in academic performance, a change in social circles, or engaging in risky behaviors such as substance use or self-harm can also be indicators of emotional distress. Parents should approach these changes with empathy, as they may reflect deeper emotional

challenges.

4. Extreme Sensitivity to Criticism: Teens often become highly sensitive to feedback during adolescence, especially from authority figures such as parents. What may seem like constructive criticism to an adult can feel like a personal attack to a teenager, triggering emotional outbursts or self-doubt.

How to Support Your Teen Through Emotional Ups and Downs

While adolescence can be a turbulent time for both teens and their parents, there are several ways that parents can support their children emotionally during this stage of life.

1. Create an Open, Non-Judgmental Environment: One of the most important things parents can do is create a safe space where their teen feels comfortable expressing their feelings. Open communication is essential. Let your child know they can talk to you about their struggles without fear of judgment or punishment. Listening actively and empathetically can go a long way in helping teens feel understood and supported.

2. Be Patient and Avoid Overreacting: Teenagers

may not always express their emotions in the most appropriate ways, but it's crucial for parents to remain calm and patient. Reacting with anger or frustration to a teen's emotional outbursts can escalate the situation and lead to further withdrawal or resistance. Instead, offer validation and understanding and avoid minimizing their feelings. Phrases like "I can see you're upset and I'm here to listen" can show your child that their feelings are taken seriously.

3. Set Boundaries with Empathy: While it's important to give teens the space to develop their independence, they still need structure and boundaries. Setting clear expectations around behavior, respect and communication can help them feel secure while also allowing them to explore their own identity. Be sure to communicate these boundaries with empathy, explaining the reasoning behind them rather than just imposing rules.

4. Encourage Healthy Coping Mechanisms: Teens often turn to unhealthy coping strategies, such as substance use or social media overuse, to manage their emotions. Encourage your teen to explore healthy outlets such as exercise, journaling or creative expression. Teach them mindfulness techniques or stress management strategies that can help them navigate emotional ups and downs.

5. Seek Professional Help if Needed: If your

teen's emotional struggles become overwhelming or persistent, don't hesitate to seek professional help. A counselor or therapist can provide your child with the tools to better understand and manage their emotions. Therapy can also be a space where teens can express themselves openly without the pressure of family dynamics.

Supporting your teen through the emotional rollercoaster of adolescence requires a combination of patience, empathy and understanding. By acknowledging the biological and psychological factors that shape teen emotions, parents can foster a supportive environment that encourages healthy emotional development. Open communication, setting appropriate boundaries and encouraging healthy coping strategies can help teens navigate the challenges of adolescence while maintaining a strong, trusting relationship with their parents.

CHAPTER FIFTEEN

ADDRESSING SOCIAL MEDIA AND SCREEN TIME: BUILDING HEALTHY DIGITAL HABITS

In the digital age, technology has brought profound changes to the way we communicate, work and even entertain ourselves. Social media platforms, smartphones and other digital devices have become integrated into daily life, offering unprecedented access to information and connectivity. However, with the rise of social media and increasing screen time, concerns about their impact on mental health, relationships and productivity have also emerged. It's crucial to address the ways in which these tools affect our well-being and to build healthier digital habits to strike a balance between connectivity and personal well-being.

The Impact of Social Media and Screen Time on Mental Health

Social media, while offering opportunities for

connection and self-expression, has been linked to several mental health issues. Studies have shown that excessive screen time and the constant exposure to curated posts can lead to feelings of inadequacy, anxiety, and depression. The comparison culture on platforms like Instagram and Facebook can amplify the pressure to conform to unrealistic standards, which may worsen self-esteem, particularly among young people.

Additionally, the dopamine-driven nature of social media, where each notification or new post is designed to grab attention, can result in addictive behaviors. This constant engagement with our devices may also disrupt sleep patterns, leading to poor sleep quality and fatigue. Sleep deprivation, in turn, exacerbates mood disorders and impairs cognitive function, further contributing to the mental toll of excessive screen time.

Social Media and Screen Time's Effects on Relationships

Relationships, whether personal or professional, can suffer due to excessive use of social media and screens. In personal relationships, the presence of smartphones during meals or conversations can lead to what's known as "phubbing" (phone snubbing), where individuals prioritize their devices over interacting with those around them. This can create feelings of neglect, resentment and disconnection, ultimately leading to relationship strain.

In a professional context, constant connectivity via social media and emails can blur the lines between work and personal life. The pressure to stay available and responsive, particularly with the rise of remote work, can lead to burnout. Social media's role in fostering unrealistic expectations of productivity, through posts that highlight achievements or workaholic lifestyles, can also contribute to stress and anxiety, as individuals may feel compelled to keep up with others.

The Importance of Healthy Digital Habits

In response to these challenges, building healthy digital habits is essential for maintaining mental health, fostering healthy relationships and enhancing productivity. Here are several steps individuals can take to manage screen time more effectively and create a more balanced relationship with technology:

Set Time Limits and Prioritize Face-to-Face Interaction

One of the first steps to curbing excessive screen time is setting clear time limits on social media and other screen-based activities. Many smartphones offer built-in features to track screen time and allow users to set daily limits for specific apps. By consciously limiting the amount of time spent on social media platforms, individuals can reclaim precious hours for other enriching activities, such as spending time with family, engaging in hobbies, or focusing on personal growth.

Additionally, prioritizing in-person interactions over digital ones can strengthen personal connections.

Although virtual interactions can be convenient, they cannot replace the emotional depth and authenticity that face-to-face conversations provide. Allocating time for meaningful offline activities, such as cooking together, going for walks, or engaging in deep, uninterrupted conversations, can help rebuild stronger, more fulfilling relationships.

Digital Detox and Mindful Consumption

Another effective strategy is implementing regular digital detoxes. A digital detox involves disconnecting from digital devices, including social media, for a set period. This can be done on a daily basis (such as taking a break from screens an hour before bed) or more extended periods, such as a weekend or vacation away from all screens. A digital detox provides an opportunity to re-center oneself, reconnect with nature, and regain focus on the present moment.

Mindful consumption of digital content is also key. Instead of mindlessly scrolling through social media, individuals can focus on engaging with content that is purposeful, uplifting, and educational. This can include following accounts that promote positive mental health, learning new skills, or connecting with communities that share meaningful interests. By curating what we consume, we can reduce exposure to negativity and foster a more positive digital environment.

Establish Boundaries Between Work and Personal Life

To combat the negative effects of technology on relationships and work-life balance, it is essential to establish clear boundaries between work and personal life. Setting designated "no tech" times, such as during meals, before bed, or on weekends, can help individuals disconnect and recharge. Similarly, creating a physical space in the home where work or personal screens are kept out of reach can help reduce the temptation to be constantly plugged in. Employers and managers also have a role in promoting healthy digital habits by encouraging employees to take breaks, disconnect after work hours and prioritize self-care. By cultivating a workplace culture that values balance and well-being, organizations can help reduce the stress and burnout that often accompany excessive screen time.

Practice Gratitude and Mindfulness

Practicing gratitude and mindfulness can counteract the anxiety and dissatisfaction that often arise from social media use. Taking a few moments each day to reflect on positive experiences, relationships and achievements can shift the focus away from what others are doing and encourage a sense of contentment. Mindfulness practices, such as meditation or mindful breathing, can also help individuals stay grounded and reduce the negative impact of digital distractions.

The pervasive role of social media and screen time in modern life has both positive and negative effects on mental health, relationships, and productivity. While it offers vast opportunities for connection and knowledge, it also brings challenges related to comparison, addiction, and burnout. By setting boundaries, practicing mindfulness, and fostering healthier digital habits, individuals can regain control over their digital lives and improve their overall well-being. It's not about rejecting technology altogether but rather about using it intentionally and in moderation to enhance, rather than hinder, our quality of life. Building these habits is an ongoing process, one that requires awareness, reflection and a commitment to a balanced and healthy relationship with the digital world.

CHAPTER SIXTEEN

PREPARING YOUR TEEN FOR ADULTHOOD: LIFE SKILLS EVERY PARENT SHOULD TEACH

As a parent, one of your most important roles is to guide your child into adulthood, helping them develop the life skills necessary to navigate the world with confidence and competence. Adolescence is a critical time for teaching practical skills that go beyond academics and instilling good habits during these formative years can set your teen up for a successful future. The following life skills are essential for preparing your teen for adulthood and as a parent, you can play a key role in ensuring that they acquire them.

Financial Literacy

Understanding personal finances is one of the most crucial life skills every teen should learn. In today's world, teens are exposed to financial concepts earlier than ever, but many still lack a solid understanding of budgeting, saving, investing, and managing debt.

Financial literacy is essential for making smart decisions when it comes to spending, saving and planning for the future.

Parents should start by teaching teens how to manage money. This includes explaining the basics of budgeting, the importance of setting financial goals, and the concept of needs versus wants. It's also important to introduce them to the idea of credit, how to avoid debt traps, and the value of saving for emergencies and long-term goals. Encourage them to open a bank account, track their spending, and use tools like budgeting apps. If appropriate, involving them in family financial decisions, such as paying bills or making large purchases, can also help them understand real-world financial responsibilities.

Time Management

As teens transition into adulthood, they will need to juggle school, work, social lives, and other commitments. Effective time management is a skill that will serve them well throughout their lives. It is not just about managing a schedule; it's about learning to prioritize tasks and balance responsibilities.

Parents can help teens develop time management skills by encouraging the use of planners or digital calendars to track commitments. Teach them how to break down large tasks into smaller, more manageable steps, and the importance of setting aside time for self-care. Additionally, it's crucial to help teens understand that time management involves saying no when necessary to avoid overloading themselves, and it's okay to ask for help when feeling overwhelmed.

Problem-Solving and Critical Thinking

Life is full of unexpected challenges, and the ability to think critically and solve problems is an invaluable skill. Encouraging teens to approach problems with an analytical mindset will help them become resourceful adults who can handle adversity effectively.

Parents can foster problem-solving skills by presenting challenges that require creative thinking and allowing their teens to come up with their own solutions. This could involve everyday situations such as troubleshooting a broken household item, solving a conflict with a friend, or managing a tough academic project. Encourage your teen to evaluate different perspectives, weigh pros and cons and think about potential outcomes before making decisions. Praise their efforts even when the solutions aren't perfect, as the goal is to build resilience and self-confidence.

Communication Skills

Being able to communicate effectively is essential for building relationships, advancing in a career, and navigating various social situations. Communication is not just about talking it's also about listening, understanding non-verbal cues and expressing oneself clearly.

To help your teen develop communication skills, engage in open and honest conversations with them.

Encourage them to express their thoughts and feelings and teach them how to listen actively. Practice empathy by discussing different perspectives and discussing how to handle conflicts respectfully. Also, it's essential to guide your teen in understanding the importance of body language, tone of voice and maintaining eye contact during conversations, as these factors can impact how messages are received. Public speaking, writing and negotiating are also helpful communication skills to develop, especially if your teen is considering a career that involves frequent interaction with others.

Self-Care and Emotional Regulation

As they enter adulthood, teens face increased pressure, stress and responsibility. Learning to manage their emotions and prioritize self-care is vital for maintaining mental and physical well-being.

Teaching your teen the importance of emotional regulation involves helping them understand their emotions and how to cope with stress in healthy ways.

Encourage your teen to practice mindfulness, meditation or deep breathing techniques when feeling anxious or overwhelmed. Additionally, ensure that they understand the value of sleep, exercise, and healthy eating in maintaining a balanced life. Setting aside time for hobbies, relaxation, and socializing with friends also promotes emotional well-being. As a parent, leading by example and demonstrating good self-care habits will reinforce the importance of this practice.

Basic Household Chores and Maintenance

Adulting isn't just about managing a career or finances; it's also about being able to take care of your living space. Teaching your teen basic household chores and maintenance is essential for fostering independence and responsibility.

Start by involving your teen in regular household tasks, such as doing laundry, cooking meals, cleaning, and organizing. Show them how to perform simple home repairs or troubleshooting tasks, such as fixing a leaky faucet or replacing a light bulb. While it may seem like a chore at the time, these skills will help your teen feel empowered to manage their own space when they leave home.

Decision Making and Responsibility

Adulthood requires making decisions that can have long-term consequences. Teaching your teen how to make informed and responsible decisions is a critical part of preparing them for life after high school.

Start by involving your teen in decisions that impact their daily lives. Encourage them to weigh the pros and cons, consider their values and think about the possible consequences of their actions. This could apply to decisions about their education, career, finances, relationships or health. Help them understand that making mistakes is part of the process, but taking responsibility for their actions and learning from them is crucial for personal growth.

Preparing your teen for adulthood requires intentional

effort, patience and guidance. By teaching them essential life skills such as financial literacy, time management, communication, emotional regulation, and household responsibilities, you are setting them up for success in the real world. These skills will not only help them become independent and self-sufficient adults but also empower them to lead fulfilling, balanced lives. As a parent, your role is to be both a teacher and a mentor, equipping your teen with the tools they need to navigate the complexities of adult life with confidence and resilience.

CHAPTER SEVENTEEN

MANAGING SIBLING RIVALRY: TURNING CONFLICT INTO COOPERATION

Sibling rivalry is a common phenomenon in many families, often occurring as children grow and develop their own individual personalities. This rivalry can manifest in various ways, from petty arguments and squabbles to more serious conflicts. While some rivalry is natural and may even be helpful in developing skills like negotiation and conflict resolution, when left unchecked, it can lead to long-term resentment and dysfunction within the family. Thus, managing sibling rivalry effectively is crucial for fostering a healthy family dynamic. This article explores strategies for turning sibling conflict into cooperation, focusing on understanding the roots of rivalry, offering practical approaches for managing it, and promoting healthier relationships among siblings.

Understanding the Roots of Sibling Rivalry

Before delving into strategies to manage sibling rivalry, it's important to understand why it occurs in the first place. Rivalry between siblings often arises from a combination of emotional, social and environmental factors.

1. Parental Attention: One of the most significant contributors to sibling rivalry is the competition for parental attention and approval. Children often feel the need to compete for the love and validation of their parents, leading to jealousy and conflict when they perceive their sibling as receiving more attention, praise or resources.
2. Personality Differences: Siblings may have different temperaments, communication styles, and interests, which can lead to misunderstandings and clashes. One child might be more extroverted and attention-seeking, while another may be quieter and more reserved. These differences can create friction, especially if the siblings struggle to understand or respect each other's individuality.
3. Birth Order: The concept of birth order can also

play a role in sibling rivalry. Older children may feel a sense of responsibility or entitlement, while younger siblings might experience frustration over being treated as the "baby" of the family. Such dynamics can lead to competition for dominance, attention and affection.

4. Perceived Inequality: Children often feel that their siblings are treated differently, whether it is in terms of discipline, reward or privileges. These perceived inequities can fuel resentment and competition, leading to a sense of unfairness that intensifies rivalry.

5. Environmental Stressors: Family stressors such as financial difficulties, parental separation, or a major life change can also exacerbate sibling rivalry. In such cases, the conflict may be a manifestation of underlying anxiety or frustration that children don't know how to express productively.

Strategies for Managing Sibling Rivalry

While sibling rivalry is a normal part of family life, managing it in a way that promotes cooperation and healthy relationships requires intentional effort. Below are several strategies that can help parents turn sibling conflict into opportunities for growth and understanding.

1. Promote Empathy and Understanding

One of the most effective ways to mitigate rivalry is by teaching children empathy. Helping siblings understand each other's perspectives can reduce conflict and promote cooperation. For example, parents can guide children to express how they feel during a conflict, while encouraging the other sibling to listen without judgment. This helps children develop an understanding of their sibling's feelings and can often reduce the intensity of arguments.

Encouraging the siblings to practice empathy not only makes them more compassionate but also helps to foster a sense of shared responsibility for maintaining peace. Parents can model empathetic behavior in their own interactions with their children and between each other, reinforcing the importance of mutual respect and understanding.

2. Create Opportunities for Positive Interaction

While conflict is inevitable, parents can also create

opportunities for siblings to bond over shared activities that require cooperation. Engaging in collaborative tasks, such as working together on a project, playing a cooperative game or cooking a meal, can build trust and strengthen relationships. These activities encourage children to rely on one another, reinforcing the idea that cooperation is more rewarding than rivalry.

Parents should also encourage siblings to spend time alone together without distractions, allowing them to build their own unique connection. Creating spaces for positive interactions helps to reduce negative patterns of behavior by shifting the focus from competition to collaboration.

3. Set Clear Expectations and Boundaries

Having clear rules and boundaries in the home is essential for managing sibling rivalry. When children understand the consequences of certain behaviors, such as name-calling, physical aggression or disrespect, they are more likely to refrain from engaging in such actions. Parents should establish consistent expectations for respectful behavior and calmly enforce these boundaries when necessary. Additionally, parents can ensure that children have their own personal space and time for individual activities, reducing feelings of territoriality that may lead to conflict. When children feel that their needs for privacy and autonomy are respected, they are less likely to engage in competitive behaviors out of frustration.

4. Encourage Teamwork, Not Competition

Many families inadvertently foster a competitive environment by focusing on winning and rewards. While some healthy competition can be motivating, it's important to emphasize the value of teamwork over individual success. For instance, if siblings are involved in a competitive activity, parents can praise their collaborative efforts rather than singling out one child as the "winner." This approach shifts the focus from rivalry to collaboration, which helps reduce jealousy and animosity.

Moreover, instead of comparing siblings' achievements, parents should celebrate each child's unique strengths and accomplishments. This practice helps to avoid the damaging effects of comparison and encourages siblings to appreciate each other's abilities rather than viewing them as rivals.

5. Model Conflict Resolution Skills

Parents play a critical role in demonstrating how to manage conflict. By modeling effective communication, problem-solving, and conflict resolution skills, parents can teach children how to navigate disputes in a healthy and constructive manner. For example, parents can show children how to express their emotions calmly, use "I" statements instead of blaming, and work together to find a solution that benefits everyone.

When parents intervene in sibling conflicts, they should avoid taking sides and instead encourage the children to resolve the issue themselves. This approach helps to empower children and fosters a sense of responsibility for resolving conflicts independently.

6. Recognize and Address Underlying Issues

Sometimes sibling rivalry is a symptom of deeper issues, such as insecurity, low self-esteem, or unmet emotional needs. In such cases, it's important for parents to recognize the root causes of conflict and address them directly. For instance, if a child feels neglected or overlooked, parents can work to ensure that each child receives individual attention and support.

By addressing underlying emotional needs, parents can help children feel more secure in their relationships with one another, reducing the need for rivalry as a way of gaining attention or validation.

Sibling rivalry is a natural part of growing up, but it doesn't have to be a destructive force in the family. With the right strategies in place, parents can turn conflict into cooperation by fostering empathy, promoting positive interactions, setting clear boundaries, encouraging teamwork, modeling conflict resolution skills and addressing underlying emotional issues. By doing so, they help siblings build stronger, more supportive relationships that will last a lifetime. With patience and consistency, sibling rivalry can evolve into a healthy dynamic of mutual respect and cooperation.

CHAPTER EIGHTEEN

PARENTING THROUGH STRESSFUL TIMES: STRATEGIES FOR RESILIENCE DURING FAMILY CHALLENGES

Parenting can be an incredibly rewarding experience, but it also comes with its own set of challenges. Every family faces difficulties, whether it's financial hardships, health crises, work-related stress or other unforeseen events. During these stressful times, the role of a parent becomes even more crucial in shaping how the family as a whole handles adversity. Parenting through stressful times requires resilience, flexibility, and a conscious effort to maintain emotional balance in the face of hardship. Here, we'll explore effective strategies that parents can use to foster resilience in their children and themselves during challenging times.

Acknowledge the Stress and Its Impact

The first step in navigating stressful times as a parent is acknowledging the stress and how it impacts both the family and individual members. It's easy to dismiss emotions or try to mask them, especially when there's a lot to juggle. However, recognizing and naming the stress is important for parents and children alike. Parents should take time to reflect on how stress is affecting their behavior, moods and responses to situations.

For children, this acknowledgment can be incredibly reassuring. It helps children understand that everyone experiences difficult feelings and that it's okay to feel anxious, sad or frustrated. By validating these emotions, parents create an environment where children feel safe to express their own concerns and worries. It is crucial to model emotional awareness to children, so they can learn healthy ways to cope with their own stress later in life.

Maintain Open Communication

One of the most important strategies in parenting through stress is fostering open communication. Keeping the lines of communication open between parents and children is essential for emotional well-being. This means not only speaking openly about the challenges the family is facing but also being a good listener. Many times, children may internalize their feelings, unsure of how to express them. Parents should create a safe, non-judgmental space where children can talk about their concerns, fears and emotions.

Parents can ask questions that encourage open dialogue, such as, "How are you feeling today?" or "What do you need from me right now?" This type of communication helps children feel supported, understood and less isolated during stressful times.

Additionally, parents should share age-appropriate information about what's happening within the family, whether it's a financial setback or a health issue.

When children understand the situation, they are less likely to feel confused or frightened. They will also learn how to manage their own emotions more effectively when they know what to expect.

Focus on Routine and Stability

In times of uncertainty, routines provide a sense of stability and normalcy. For children, structure can be particularly comforting when everything around them feels unpredictable. Maintaining a consistent daily routine, such as regular meal times, bedtimes and family activities, can help reduce anxiety and provide children with a sense of control.

Parents should aim to create predictable patterns even in the midst of chaos. If there are major disruptions to the family's usual routine, such as a parent losing a job or a change in the family's living situation, it's important to establish new routines as quickly as possible. Having a sense of structure allows children to know what to expect, which can make them feel more secure.

Moreover, routines don't just benefit children; they also offer parents a sense of predictability in their day-to-day lives. This predictability can help parents cope with their own stress and avoid becoming overwhelmed.

Prioritize Self-Care

Resilient parenting is not only about caring for children; it's also about taking care of oneself. Parents need to recognize that their well-being is closely tied to their ability to support their children. Self-care doesn't mean neglecting responsibilities but rather ensuring that parents are in a good physical, emotional and mental state to be there for their children.

Self-care can take many forms: getting enough sleep, engaging in physical activity, maintaining healthy eating habits, seeking emotional support from friends or professionals and allowing time for relaxation. It's also important for parents to seek out moments of solitude when needed, even if it's just a few minutes of quiet in a busy day.

When parents prioritize self-care, they model healthy habits for their children. They demonstrate that taking care of one's mental and physical health is not selfish but essential, particularly in times of stress. By doing so, parents show children that it's okay to take a break when needed and that they have the power to manage their stress in constructive ways.

Foster Flexibility and Adaptability

While routines are important, it's also essential to remain flexible and adaptable when things don't go as planned. Stressful times often bring unexpected challenges that require creative problem-solving and the ability to adjust expectations. Teaching children to be adaptable in the face of change is a key life skill that will help them build resilience.

Parents can model flexibility by showing how to cope with setbacks in a calm and constructive way. For example, if a parent has to cancel plans due to a work commitment or a family emergency, they can explain the situation and offer alternative ways to enjoy family time. By focusing on solutions rather than dwelling on the problem, parents help children see that challenges can be overcome with a positive mindset.

Flexibility also involves adjusting expectations. Parents should be kind to themselves and avoid placing unrealistic demands on their own performance. Stressful times are not the best time to strive for perfection; instead, parents should focus on doing their best while being compassionate toward themselves and their children.

Encourage Resilience through Positive Coping Strategies

Resilience is the ability to bounce back from adversity, and parents can help children develop this skill by modeling positive coping strategies. These strategies might include deep breathing exercises, mindfulness techniques, engaging in creative activities like art or journaling or finding ways to connect with nature. When parents introduce these coping strategies into their family life, children learn that they have the tools to navigate difficult situations.

It's also helpful for parents to frame challenges as opportunities for growth. For example, instead of viewing a setback as something purely negative, parents can reframe it as a chance to learn resilience or problem-solving skills. This positive mindset encourages children to approach difficulties with an optimistic outlook and the belief that they can overcome obstacles.

Stay Connected with Support Systems

Finally, no parent should feel that they have to navigate stressful times alone. Building and maintaining strong support networks is key to resilience. Whether it's relying on family, friends or community resources, having a support system can make a world of difference when it comes to managing stress.

Parents should feel comfortable reaching out for help when needed. This might mean asking a friend for emotional support, seeking professional counseling, or even relying on a local community organization for assistance. When parents show that it's okay to ask for help, they teach their children an invaluable lesson about the importance of seeking support when facing challenges.

Parenting through stressful times requires a delicate balance of strength and flexibility. By acknowledging the stress, maintaining open communication, prioritizing routines and self-care, fostering adaptability and modeling positive coping strategies, parents can help their families navigate challenges with resilience. With these strategies, both parents and children can emerge stronger, more connected and better equipped to handle the inevitable ups and downs of life.

CHAPTER NINETEEN

THE ROLE OF SELF-CARE IN PARENTING: PRIORITIZING YOUR WELL-BEING TO BETTER SUPPORT YOUR CHILD

Parenting is one of the most rewarding yet challenging experiences in life. It requires constant attention, patience, and energy to meet the emotional, physical, and psychological needs of a child. While parents often focus on the well-being of their children, it is equally important to prioritize their own health and happiness. Self-care, often viewed as a personal luxury or indulgence, is an essential component of effective parenting. By taking care of oneself, parents are better equipped to support their children in a healthy, balanced way. This essay explores the importance of self-care in parenting, its impact on parents and children and practical strategies parents can implement to prioritize their well-being.

Understanding the Concept of Self-Care

Self-care refers to the intentional actions taken to promote and maintain one's physical, mental and emotional health. It is not simply about pampering oneself, but rather about engaging in regular activities that nourish the body and mind. These activities may include exercise, healthy eating, engaging in hobbies, mindfulness practices and ensuring adequate rest and relaxation. In the context of parenting, self-care becomes an essential tool for parents to sustain their energy levels, manage stress and model healthy behaviors for their children.

The Relationship Between Self-Care and Effective Parenting

When parents take the time to care for their own needs, they are better able to meet the needs of their children. Parenting can be physically and emotionally exhausting, and neglecting personal well-being can lead to burnout. Self-care helps prevent this by offering parents a chance to recharge and reflect.

Parents who engage in self-care are typically less irritable, more patient, and more emotionally available for their children. These qualities are essential in fostering a positive, nurturing environment where children can thrive.

Moreover, practicing self-care encourages emotional regulation. Parents who take care of their mental health are more likely to manage stress effectively and avoid reacting impulsively to challenging parenting situations. This emotional balance is crucial in parenting, as it enables parents to respond to their children's behavior with empathy and understanding, rather than frustration or anger.

Modeling Self-Care for Children

Children learn by example. When parents engage in self-care practices, they send a powerful message to their children about the importance of taking care of one's body and mind. This modeling helps children develop healthy habits and an understanding of the value of self-care from a young age. For instance, a parent who prioritizes physical exercise, such as going for a walk or practicing yoga, can instill in their child the importance of physical activity. Similarly, parents who take time for mental health care, such as practicing mindfulness or engaging in hobbies, teach their children the importance of managing emotions and stress.

As children grow, they will likely encounter various challenges, such as academic pressures, peer relationships and emotional struggles. By seeing their parents prioritize self-care, they can learn healthy coping strategies and understand that taking care of themselves is not a sign of selfishness but a necessary part of life. This understanding can help children grow into emotionally resilient adults who are more adept at managing their own well-being.

Reducing Parental Burnout

Parental burnout is a growing concern, particularly in today's fast-paced and demanding world. When parents neglect their own needs and focus solely on their children, they may experience feelings of exhaustion, frustration and a sense of being overwhelmed. This can result in a diminished ability to care for their child's emotional and physical needs. In contrast, self-care helps parents avoid burnout by promoting a balanced lifestyle.

Self-care activities provide a necessary break from the demands of parenting, offering parents time to reconnect with themselves and recharge. This respite allows them to return to their parenting duties with renewed energy and focus. Whether through a simple act like taking a few minutes to meditate, engaging in a hobby, or enjoying a day out with friends, self-care helps parents refresh their mental and emotional batteries. This not only improves the quality of care they provide to their children but also contributes to their overall happiness and life satisfaction.

Self-Care as a Tool for Stress Management

Parenting often involves high levels of stress, especially when juggling multiple responsibilities.

Financial pressures, work-life balance, household chores, and the emotional demands of raising children can be overwhelming. Stress, if left unchecked, can have detrimental effects on both parents and children, leading to negative physical and mental health outcomes. Practicing self-care can be an effective tool for managing stress.

One of the key aspects of self-care is stress reduction. Activities like deep breathing exercises, meditation or spending time in nature can lower stress levels and promote relaxation. Parents who regularly engage in such practices are better equipped to handle difficult parenting moments, such as tantrums or sibling conflicts, with a calm and measured approach. In this way, self-care enables parents to maintain a sense of control and emotional clarity, which benefits both their well-being and their children's emotional development.

Practical Self-Care Strategies for Parents

While the concept of self-care may seem simple,

finding the time and energy to implement it as a parent can be challenging. However, there are several practical strategies that parents can use to prioritize their well-being:

1. Set Boundaries: Establishing clear boundaries between personal time and family time is essential for self-care. Parents should learn to say no when they are overwhelmed and make space for their own needs without feeling guilty.
2. Practice Mindfulness: Mindfulness practices, such as meditation or breathing exercises, can help parents reduce stress and stay present in the moment. Even five minutes of mindful breathing can have a significant impact on mental clarity.
3. Delegate and Ask for Help: Parenting does not have to be done alone. Asking for help from a partner, family members or friends can provide much-needed relief. Delegating tasks allows parents to focus on their self-care without feeling the burden of doing everything themselves.
4. Make Time for Hobbies: Engaging in activities that bring joy, such as reading, painting, or gardening, can provide an emotional outlet for parents. Hobbies help parents reconnect with their passions and offer a break from the routine of parenting.

5. Physical Exercise: Regular physical activity is one of the most effective ways to boost both physical and mental health. Parents should find time to exercise, whether through a morning walk, yoga session, or family bike ride.

Self-care is a critical component of effective parenting. By prioritizing their own well-being, parents are better able to manage stress, avoid burnout and model healthy behaviors for their children. Taking time for self-care enables parents to be more present, patient and emotionally available for their children, ultimately fostering a supportive and nurturing environment. Parenting is a lifelong journey and by making self-care a priority, parents can sustain their energy, happiness and well-being, allowing them to be the best possible caregivers for their children.

CHAPTER TWENTY

PARENTING AS A TEAM: HOW TO ALIGN WITH YOUR PARTNER FOR CONSISTENT GUIDANCE

Parenting is one of the most significant roles in life, but it can also be one of the most challenging. The demands of raising children, managing schedules, and balancing responsibilities can sometimes create tension between partners. However, when parents work together as a team, they can provide more consistent and supportive guidance to their children, fostering a healthy family dynamic. The key to effective co-parenting lies in alignment, communication and shared goals. Below are some ways to align with your partner for consistent guidance in parenting.

Establish Clear, Shared Values and Parenting Goals

The first step toward becoming a united parenting team is to establish shared values and goals. Parents must be on the same page about what they want for their children and what values they wish to instill in them. These values could range from how children should behave in social situations to their approach toward education or even discipline.

It's essential that both partners have a conversation about what is most important to them in raising their children. These discussions might address topics like respect, independence, empathy, or kindness. Parents should also talk about what kind of behavior is acceptable and what is not, and how they both envision the overall development of their children.

Having shared goals will provide a solid foundation that both parents can rely on, especially in moments of disagreement. When situations arise where one parent feels strongly about a particular course of action, it's helpful to refer back to these established values to ensure decisions are aligned with the family's overarching goals.

Communicate Openly and Regularly

Communication is the cornerstone of any healthy relationship, especially when it comes to parenting. Parents need to talk openly and regularly about their children's progress, behavior, and any issues that arise. It's not enough to discuss parenting only when a problem arises; continuous, honest communication about the day-to-day experiences of parenting helps parents stay aligned and united.

A good way to keep communication strong is by scheduling regular check-ins with each other. These can be informal, such as during a walk after dinner, or more structured, like a weekly "parenting meeting" where you discuss the week's successes and challenges. This gives both parents an opportunity to voice concerns, share victories and adjust their strategies as needed.

It's important to remember that communication is not

just about expressing opinions but also about active listening. Make sure each parent feels heard and understood. When one parent is frustrated, the other should listen without jumping to conclusions or offering immediate solutions. This open dialogue can help foster understanding and strengthen the partnership.

Divide Responsibilities and Respect Each Other's Roles

In many households, one parent may take on more of the caregiving or household duties, while the other might be more focused on providing financially or managing certain aspects of the family dynamic. However, parenting requires more than just division of labor—it requires mutual respect for each other's roles and efforts.

Both parents should acknowledge and respect each other's unique contributions to the family. For instance, if one parent stays at home while the other works, the parent at home may face different challenges than the one who is at work. Conversely, the working parent might be feeling the pressure of providing financially. Each parent should acknowledge the pressures the other faces, showing empathy and support.

It's also crucial to divide parenting duties in a way that makes sense for your family. This means not only dividing tasks based on availability but also strengths. One parent may be better at helping with homework, while the other might have more patience during bedtime routines. Balancing these strengths ensures that both parents are empowered and that their children benefit from both types of parenting.

Work Together on Discipline and Boundaries

One of the most critical areas where consistency is needed in parenting is discipline. Children thrive on routine and clear boundaries, so it's essential for both parents to be in sync when it comes to discipline. This doesn't mean that both parents need to have identical approaches, but they should have a shared understanding of what behaviors are acceptable and what consequences will follow if those behaviors are violated.

Before taking disciplinary action, parents should have a discussion about what methods will work best in their household. This could involve setting clear and consistent rules for things like screen time, chores, bedtime, and behavior expectations. When both parents are on the same page regarding consequences and rewards, children are less likely to test boundaries.

Consistency is key to effective discipline. If one parent is overly lenient while the other is more strict, children may become confused about what is expected of them. By maintaining a united front, parents are providing their children with the structure and stability they need to feel secure.

Support Each Other and Avoid Undermining

Parenting can be exhausting, and it's natural to feel frustrated or overwhelmed at times. When one parent is feeling exhausted or has reached their breaking point, the other should step in and offer support. This could mean taking over certain responsibilities, giving the other parent a break or simply providing moral support.

It's important that parents also avoid undermining each other, especially in front of the children. If one parent makes a decision or sets a rule, the other should refrain from contradicting or over-riding that decision immediately. This can confuse children and lead to a lack of respect for the authority of both parents. Instead, parents should discuss differences privately and come to a consensus. This way, the children see their parents as a united team.

Adapt and Evolve as a Team

Parenting is a dynamic experience and as children

grow and change, so too should parenting strategies. What worked for a toddler may not be effective with a teenager, and what worked with one child may not work with another. Therefore, parents must be willing to adapt their approach and evolve as a team.

Both partners should regularly reflect on their parenting practices and be open to making changes when necessary. This might mean reevaluating rules, adjusting expectations, or trying new strategies to support each other and their children. Parenting as a team requires flexibility and a willingness to learn and grow together.

Parenting is not a solo task; it's a partnership that requires communication, alignment and mutual support. When parents work together as a cohesive team, they provide their children with the stability, love and guidance they need to thrive. By setting shared values, dividing responsibilities, maintaining open communication and supporting each other, parents can create a harmonious environment that fosters consistent guidance for their children's development. The key to successful co-parenting lies not just in the ability to parent individually but in the commitment to working together for the good of the whole family.

CONCLUSION

"Parenting Guide Made Simple: Proven Strategies to Navigate Every Stage of Your Child's Growth" by George Martin offers a comprehensive and practical approach to raising children through various stages of development, from infancy to adolescence. The book is designed to help parents understand and address the evolving needs of their children, providing valuable strategies for creating a nurturing, supportive environment at each age. The author combines psychological insights with practical advice, making the book an essential resource for both new and experienced parents. Below is a summary of the key concepts from the book's structure, which is divided into five sections.

Section 1: Foundations of Effective Parenting
The first section emphasizes the importance of laying a strong foundation for parenting. Martin begins by helping parents understand their parenting style,

explaining how different styles impact a child's development. The book highlights the significance of a secure parent-child bond, which is crucial for building trust and providing emotional safety. One of the central themes here is active listening, which encourages parents to communicate effectively and empathetically with their children. Martin also discusses the difference between discipline and punishment, stressing the importance of positive discipline techniques that guide behavior rather than simply imposing consequences.

Section 2: Early Childhood (0-5 Years)

In the second section, Martin addresses the critical early years of a child's life. He explains how nurturing emotional intelligence in toddlers helps them develop essential social skills, preparing them for future interactions. The book provides strategies for handling tantrums, teaching parents how to remain calm and patient in the face of emotional outbursts. Play is another key focus, with Martin exploring how creative and educational play supports cognitive and social development. Establishing routines during this stage is also emphasized, as predictable schedules offer children a sense of security and confidence as they navigate the world around them.

Section 3: Middle Childhood (6-12 Years)

As children grow older, their needs and challenges evolve. In this section, Martin explores how to foster independence in children, helping them explore and learn while maintaining safety. He discusses the importance of instilling values such as kindness, responsibility, and respect, which are essential for shaping a child's character. Martin also provides insights into navigating peer relationships and the dynamics of friendships, guiding parents on how to support their child's social development. The book emphasizes the importance of academic support, encouraging a love for learning while avoiding the pressure that can stifle a child's natural curiosity.

Section 4: The Teenage Years (13-18 Years)

Adolescence is often the most challenging stage of parenting, and Martin provides valuable guidance on how to navigate this period. One of the key themes in this section is how to strike a balance between allowing teens the independence they crave while maintaining appropriate boundaries. The author also explores the emotional complexities of adolescence, offering strategies for understanding and supporting teen emotions. With the increasing presence of digital media, Martin provides practical advice on managing screen time and promoting healthy digital habits. Finally, the section covers the importance of preparing teens for adulthood by teaching essential life skills such as financial management, responsibility and decision-making.

Section 5: Parenting Challenges and Solutions

The final section of the book addresses common parenting challenges and offers solutions for overcoming them. Martin delves into managing sibling rivalry, offering strategies for turning conflict into cooperation and teaching children to resolve disputes constructively. He also provides advice on parenting through stressful times, such as family crises or personal struggles, encouraging parents to build resilience within themselves and their children. The role of self-care in parenting is another critical topic, reminding parents that maintaining their own well-being is essential for providing the best support to their children. Lastly, Martin emphasizes the importance of parenting as a team, encouraging parents to align their approaches and provide consistent guidance.

Overall, "Parenting Guide Made Simple" offers a wealth of practical advice, grounded in psychological principles, to help parents navigate the complexities of child development. With clear, actionable strategies for every stage of a child's life, the book provides a roadmap for raising emotionally healthy, well-adjusted children.